ANDRIZO

A CALL TO DISTINCTIVE & AUTHENTIC MANHOOD

MAN

1 Cor. 16:13

Foreword by Dr. Mike Hayes

JAMES DEMELO

outskirts
press

Outskirts Press, Inc.
http://www.outskirtspress.com

ISBN: 978-1-9772-0516-2

Library of Congress Control Number: 2018123456

Cover Photo - Jasen Roman

Outskirts Press and the "OP" logo are trademarks belonging to Outskirts Press, Inc.

PRINTED IN THE UNITED STATES OF AMERICA

"James deMelo is a good friend of mine and a great man of God. He has been leading men for many years, and I'm so glad he has written this powerful book. I highly recommend it as an inspiring and educational call to authentic manhood."

— Jimmy Evans
Pastor, Author, and Founder of "Marriage Today"

It is a privilege to endorse James deMelo's new book on manhood. If anyone has a right to address this issue, it is James — and in this book, he covers so many details of what it means to be a man that God cherishes in the world today. I read every word in every chapter with great enjoyment, thinking of how this book — written by a real man — will be such a strength and encouragement to so many men who truly long to be the kind of man God wants them to be! Read this book with an open heart and courage. It will challenge you to step forward and be more than you are!

— Rick Renner
Senior Pastor, Author, Good News Church,
Moscow, Russia

"I believe James' book will inspire us to Christ-like manhood in an age where selfishness and absenteeism of fathers prevail."

— Duane VanderKlok
Senior Pastor, Resurrection Life Church,
Grandville, Michigan

"James deMelo has written the book you are holding in order to invest the years of success he's racked up from being an athlete, friend, and pastor. Those intent on reading about success but who have no intention of bettering themselves need not read this, but ANY MAN who wants to break the relentless cycle of no forward motion in his life SHOULD READ THIS. The answer has left the station and is in your hands right now."

— Brett F. Jones
Senior Pastor, Grace Church, Houston, Texas

"This is an important and powerful work. Our nation hungers for a mass transformation of males into great men. This is a must read for every man. Game changer!"

— Gordon Banks
Former NFL Player, Senior Pastor, Overcomer Covenant Church, Seattle, Washington

"My respect for James has always been massive due to what he's accomplished in his life as an athlete, family man, and minister. Now that he has brought these strong traits to us in Andrizo Man, every man has access to the tools which allow them to tap into the courageous principles of manhood that are needed in culture today."

— Steve Alessi
Senior Pastor, Metro Life Church, Miami, Florida

"The adventure Pastor James will take you on in this book has the potential to save your life, marriage, and destiny. All men need this book! Personal stories, great quotes, and scriptures are used masterfully to paint a picture of true manhood."

— Paul Ruzinsky
Senior Pastor, Resonate Church, Newaygo, Michigan

DEDICATION

This book is first dedicated to my wife, Misty, without whom I would not be the man I am today. I also dedicate this book to the many great men whom God sent into my life to model true manhood: Ed Cole, Keith Craft, Duane Vanderklok, Mike Hayes, Rick Renner, Jimmy Evans, Greg Wark, Jim Willoughby and Tim Bagwell. And last, but not least, without the support of my three incredible daughters, Alexa, Mikayla, and Elissa, I would have never understood life, sacrifice, and love as I do now.

Table of Contents

Preface

In his book, *The Last Roar,* Bob Briner wrote, "It's important that we understand that all the problems besetting our society and so-called Christians are problems of the heart. They are not institutional problems, structural, programmatic or organizational problems. They flow from individual hearts. The only way to attack wickedness successfully is with the power and love of the message of Christ directed at human hearts. Any other way will fail."

The heart is worth protecting because what's in your heart will determine your behavior, your relationships, and your future. The Old Testament prophet said, *"The heart is deceitful above all things, and it is exceedingly perverse and corrupt and severely, mortally sick! Who can know it [perceive, understand, be acquainted with his own heart and mind]?"* (Jeremiah 17:9 AMP).

In the book of Genesis, the story of Adam and Eve exposes the deception from Satan that there is "more" to experience than what they see. This "more malady," as I call it, is what many men are pursuing instead of what God truly offers. Men today feel that there has got to be more: more sex, more euphoria, more wealth, more knowledge, more respect, more power, more freedom, more testosterone. The heart of man is easily deceived by the lies of this world, and men can only find truth and authentic freedom through the knowledge of God and submission and obedience to Him.

I believe this book will help you discern your heart and "unfollow" it. The heart cannot be trusted; this is why King Solomon, the wisest man in history, said, "Guard your heart with all diligence for out of it flows the issues of life" (Proverbs 4:23). Discerning men follow their spirit and find life, honor, and righteousness. They learn that more is not always better. What is truly good and right comes from God. The heart has issues that need to be led by the Spirit of God. The Spirit helps us understand why we do what we do.

Why is it that we as men go to strange women, porn, drugs, or alcohol for relief? Why is it that no matter how successful, intelligent, or strong we believe we are, we still struggle with insecurities that end up destroying our lives? Why do we believe the lie that there is more that God is holding out on us?

Man, from the beginning of time, has wandered off God's plan and His path. We have easily gotten lost, but we have also experienced the great love and mercy of God calling us back home. The quintessential question God asked the first created man was, "Adam, where are you?" Adam was lost. Men are lost! They need to be "found," and God is the only one who can do that. Of course, when God asks a question, an answer is in order. Adam went on to explain his fears and shame of being naked and how he partook of the tree of more -"knowledge of good and evil" (Genesis 3:1-12 NKJV). God's next question was just as powerful, "Who told you that?" Of course, this question merits an answer too. Adam proceeded to blame the woman that God had given him. He did not focus on his own rebellion and his search for more. He blamed Eve, and ultimately, he blamed God. This departure from God's path always leads to confusion, hopelessness, and unnecessary pain.

I do want to note, however, that sometimes we experience episodes of tragedy that we cannot explain.

One thing we know is that from the beginning of time, Satan, the enemy, has worked and deceived to pull us off course. But when God intervenes, we live and we thrive.

I'll discuss more about this story in chapter seven, but I think it is important to mention here that God had a destiny for me even when Satan was working to destroy me, and God has one for you too. Each day we live, we encounter the battle of being pulled off course and being committed to staying on course. Sometimes we face attacks against our very physical bodies and our mental selves. I'm referring to my accident when an 18-wheeler t-boned me in a highway intersection in northern Michigan. I was thirty-five years old, and it seemed that my life was over. But God was in the plans, and even though I died for a brief moment, I am yet alive to talk about God's faithfulness, grace, mercy, and determination to see that I complete the good work that He began in me. God also has a purpose and plan for you. I intend in this book to help you see that more clearly.

I want to share with you through this book some critically important principles for restoring men's relationship—principles which Christ came to reveal to us. There is more, but it can only be found in Christ when we hear and answer His call to distinctive and authentic manhood.

Acknowledgments

There have been many readers and individuals that have made this book possible. My good friends and editors, Tony McWilliams, Richard Davis, and Kevin Herrin have provided a wealth of wisdom and guidance; without them, I'm not sure if it would have been possible. Their editing skills and book publishing expertise have been a tremendous help. Men and women like Paul Panquerne, Doug Sweet, Me Ra, and Brian Tausend all were instrumental in encouraging me to write this book. Also, my friend, Duncan Brannan, first exposed me to the phrase *"Play The Man"* that inspired me to the deepest core of my manhood.

Authors like Edwin Louis Cole, Mike Hayes, John Eldredge, Mark Batterson, Erwin McManus, Stephen

Mansfield, Bob Goff, Bob Sorge, and Brett McKay have all provided great inspiration and resources. Finally, the generosity and optimism of my brother, Joseph deMelo, has been unmatched.

Thank you!

Foreword

"Without a doubt, one of the greatest concerns for the survival of our society is the lost vision of what a real man is designed by God to look like. We hear much about divorce, fatherlessness, high prison population, rampant pornography and mistreatment of women. All of these challenges can be laid at the feet of men who are ill-equipped and often misled in our understanding of godly, authentic manhood.

Author James deMelo has brought into clear focus the vision the Father has for His men. Andrizo was a word most of us had never heard, and now thousands of men are living the Andrizo life as men of God. The Return, a four-day intensive retreat for men held at the Haven Oaks Ranch north of Dallas is where the

Andrizo life has been taught, trained and exemplified by James and his team. Over 3,000 men at the time of this writing have attended and have seen their lives transformed. I won't try to explain the Andrizo life in this foreword. I will only highly recommend that you read, devour and master the lifestyle espoused and explained in this life-changing book. My thanks to James for writing it and making it available to all who desire transformation. My challenge to you is to read it and receive its message. My prayer is that there be a generation of world-changing men raised up to take their place among the great men of history. Andrizo!"

— Mike Hayes
Founding Pastor and Author,
Covenant Church, Carrollton, Texas

Introduction

Have you ever been lost, really lost? Being lost is one of the scariest and most emotional experiences you will ever encounter. At first you think all is ok; you will figure it out, but then you realize it's not ok. The feeling of panic is overwhelming. You start to think of all the things you could have done to prevent it. You look for familiar sights, sounds, and smells to help find the way back. You beat yourself up: "You idiot, what were you thinking?" Then there are the voices to deal with, "You're not going to make, it's over!" or "Don't quit, keep moving, looking, and searching. You will find a way." The voice we listen to will determine the outcome.

This book is about being lost and finding your way back home. To me being lost meant that I had the wrong understanding of what true manhood meant. I lost it along the way in my attempts to achieve fame, fortune, and superhuman size and strength . You see, I was a well known national competitive bodybuilder who turned preacher. My journey from bodybuilding to Spirit-building is part of this book, but mostly it's about going from being a typical male to being a man. I became lost in the lie that a man has certain things, does certain things, and is certain things. He has to have women, money, muscles and power.

It wasn't until everything came crashing down that I discovered what I call "distinctive and authentic manhood." As a pastor today I have devoted my life to helping men find that path. My prayer is that this book will help you recognize God's encouraging voice and His call to "distinctive and authentic manhood."

That's What Brothers Do

C.S. Lewis once said, "One road leads home and a thousand roads lead into the wilderness."

A Brick to the Head

I grew up with two older brothers, and they could be mean at times, but I never doubted their love for me. Even when they were shooting me with pellet guns and pulling my swimming trunks off at the lake. Yes, these were my brothers—yet when it came to helping me when in trouble they were there, protecting me, willing to die for me. My brother, Johnny, is the oldest and he became a Green Beret, special forces division of the Army. He was my hero growing up. He was stationed at Fort Bragg, North Carolina, and I spent many summers with him there. He told me lots of stories about him and my middle brother, Joseph, when they were growing up. Included among those stories was the one when he and Joseph were kids. A bully started picking on Joseph and threatened to hit him with a brick. When Johnny saw it, he jumped in only to take the full impact of the brick upon his head. After he regained consciousness and assured Joseph he was not dead, their bond strengthened. Joseph has a tattoo of an eagle holding a brick with the words engraved in Portuguese, "My brother."

Another time when they were scuba diving, they were caught in an undercurrent that began to sweep them out to sea. Johnny, the stronger swimmer of the two, could swim out but Joseph succumbed to exhaustion and began to give up. He told Johnny to save himself and leave. That's when Johnny said, "I will not leave you," and grabbed him and swam them both to safety. That's what brothers do! They come to each other's aid. They go after them and seek them until they find them and bring them home to the loving arms of family, friends, and most of all, the Father.

A Brother Lost and Found

Years ago, my brother Joseph fell into despair and "went off the deep end" with drugs. He disappeared for weeks. No one could find him. I took time off work and flew to the town where he was last seen, and through much prayer and grace, I found him. When I first saw him, my heart broke. He looked like he hadn't slept in days. His eyes were sunken in with deep dark shadows. An otherwise strong-bodied and well-kept man, he was now gangly, thin, and disheveled. He smelled like a garbage dumpster even though he tried to cover it up with cologne. When our eyes first met, I saw nothing but shame and guilt in his eyes. With his head hanging down he asked, "What are you doing here?"

"Getting you home."

"Why are you doing this?"

I said, "Because that's what brothers do!"

What brothers do is help each other find the road back home. I gave him an ultimatum, "You can come with me, standing or lying down, but one way or the other you're coming home with me." He chose the latter.

It Can't End This Way

Once, while hunting in Alaska, I found myself caught in a fierce snowstorm called a "whiteout." Up until this point, I had not been around snow much and had never heard of a whiteout. To best describe what it feels like, imagine someone putting you inside a snow globe, turning it upside down and violently shaking it. There was so much snow that day I didn't know what was up or down. I could barely see my hands in front of me. The last thing the guide said most imperatively was, "Don't get off the road. Stay on the road."

But I had been following animal tracks and had gotten off the main logging road and into the woods with the thought that I could follow my own tracks back. When the snow first began to fall, it was a light snowfall. I thought I would be fine because I could still see my tracks, but before long the snow began falling heavier. This caused my tracks to disappear. I knew if I didn't find the road soon, I was in real trouble.

I didn't realize how far into the woods I traveled. What seemed a few hundred yards and an easy path back to the road had turned into two hours of dredging through knee-deep snow, tripping over logs and falling into armpit-deep bogs. I'd walked into a frozen swamp and didn't know it. I had no flares, no phone, no GPS or compass. Therefore, I lost my sense of direction. As far as I knew, I could have been walking in circles. At one point I became so exhausted and scared I prayed, "Father, please don't let me die this way. It can't end this way! Help me find my way back to the road."

I remembered I had my gun and thought, "Maybe if I fire off a round, someone will hear it." I pointed the gun in the air and pulled the trigger. To my shock, it sounded like I stuck the barrel into a thousand pillows. The snow was so thick; it muffled the sound. I tried it again with the same result. I then began to sweat, which would turn into a chill and the shakes. I knew if I didn't find the road soon, the danger of hypothermia could become my reality. That's when it happened. The road—I stepped onto the road.

I still wasn't sure what direction I needed to go, but it improved my chances and made it a whole lot better than trudging around in that frozen swamp. After walking for what seemed an eternity, I saw snowmobile headlights and a frantic-looking guide. After scolding me, he gave me a big hug and said he was on his way to get a search party when he spotted me. I have never wanted to kiss a guide before, but I was tempted to kiss this one.

I tell you this story because this book is also about a road — a road many men have lost track of in a blizzard of confusion about what real manhood looks like.

Chris Stefanick, speaker and author, says,

> *"We live in a world where manhood is defined by wealth, power, sexual potency and notoriety. Ironically, we also live in a world that tells us to undervalue all things masculine. We are almost ashamed of being men. 'We don't need your authority or masculinity or protection or deep voice, or testosterone-saturated bodies they say and, thanks to modern technology, we don't even need you to have a kid. We can go to a sperm bank for that. In other words, you're not wanted or necessary.' Is it any wonder that there is a manhood crisis? Is there any wonder that in some studies there are 25 percent more women than men in churches on any given Sunday? That over 34 percent of kids live apart from their biological dads? That*

40 percent of them haven't seen their dads in a year? That 40 percent of children live with single moms? Is there any wonder 28 percent of men say they cheated on their wives? In short, we have a generation of men that have simply checked out of authentic manhood."

This is what the book is about—brotherhood. It is about being and having someone there to help you get back on the path of distinctive and authentic manhood. It's about returning to the source of our true identity as men, and NO, it's not found in *G.Q. Magazine* or *Men's Fitness* or UFC fight nights, but in the ancient path Christ left us. That's where we will find authentic and distinctive manhood. Jeremiah, a prophet of old, spoke of this path when he wrote, *"Go stand at the crossroads and look around. Ask for directions to the old road, the tried and true road. Then take it. Discover the right route for your souls"* (Jeremiah 6:16 MSG). This book is about those crossroads, places, and moments where all men find themselves when they search for meaning, purpose, and true masculinity.

In the book of Genesis, Adam walked with God in the purest state of masculinity, intimacy, and transparency. There was no shame, no fear, and no hiding because the road was clear of bogs and logs. The swamp of sin's debris had not entered the scene. Adam's manhood needed no defining as it was authentic from the beginning. No counterfeit existed in contrast and no false persona to skew its image. It was manhood at its best!

One day that all changed.

The path became blurry; sin had entered. Man had wandered off the tried and true path. Now a thousand trails disperse manhood into the wilderness of undefined, immature, and insecure men. My goal is to help men find that road back home, where God and man can walk together, uninhibited by sin and the world's lies about manhood. This book is about my journey to find those paths or virtues. After decades of ministering to men and seeing the debris of devastation this world has inflicted on men, I sought God's heart for the answer to man's restoration to the first relationship Adam had with God—a path he lost but that Christ gave us back. The first place He led me involved the ancient story Jesus shared known as "The Lost Son" in the gospel of Luke. It really should be called "The Tale of Two Brothers" because there are two men in this story that I will showcase in this book. Ultimately it is a story of the restoration of manhood and of God's Father heart toward man. I also will bring back an ancient war cry the Apostle Paul mentions to his men in the city of Corinth. This call or war cry, mixed with five magnificent manhood virtues, changed my life and many of the men I minister to throughout the world.

2

The Tale of Two Brothers

"People live not only alongside one another, but also in manifold relationship. They live for each other; relating to one another. They are brothers and sisters."

—St. John Paul II

T he story begins with Jesus sharing this parable about these two brothers who perceived their relationship with their father in different ways. Let's pick up the story as it is recorded by Luke, a physician, and disciple of Christ,

> *"There was a man who had two sons. The younger one said to his father, 'Father, give me my share of the estate.' So, he divided his property between them. Not long after that, the younger son got together all he had, set off for a distant country and there squandered his wealth in wild living. After he had spent*

everything, there was a severe famine in that whole country, and he began to be in need. So, he went and hired himself out to a citizen of that country, who sent him to his fields to feed pigs. He longed to fill his stomach with the pods that the pigs were eating, but no one gave him anything. When he came to his senses, he said, 'How many of my father's hired servants have food to spare, and here I am starving to death! I will set out and go back to my father and say to him: Father, I have sinned against heaven and against you. I am no longer worthy to be called your son; make me like one of your hired servants.' So, he got up and went to his father. But while he was still a long way off, his father saw him and was filled with compassion for him; he ran to his son, threw his arms around him and kissed him. The son said to him, 'Father, I have sinned against heaven and against you. I am no longer worthy to be called your son.' But the father said to his servants, 'Quick! Bring the best robe and put it on him. Put a ring on his finger and sandals on his feet. Bring the fattened calf and kill it. Let's have a feast and celebrate. For this son of mine was dead and is alive again; he was lost and is found.' So, they began to celebrate. Meanwhile, the *older son was in the field. When he came near the house, he heard music and dancing. So, he called one of the servants and asked him what was going on. 'Your brother has come,' he replied, 'and your father has killed the fattened calf because he has him back safe and sound.' The older brother became angry and refused to go in. So, his father went out and pleaded with him. But he answered his father, 'Look! All these years I've been slaving for you and never disobeyed your orders. Yet you never gave me even a young goat so I could celebrate with my friends. But when this son of yours who has squandered your property with prostitutes comes home, you kill the fattened calf for him!' 'My son,' the father said, 'you are always with me, and everything I have is yours. But we had to celebrate and be glad because this brother of yours was dead and is alive again; he was lost and is found'"* (Luke 15:11-32 NIV).

No one knows why Jesus shared this story or if it was a true story that he witnessed. What we do know is this is one of three parables he shared about lost things found and the joy it brings. The fact that he shared it makes it worthy of our attention. I believe the reason God the Father led me to this story and why it became the heart and soul of our extremely successful men's retreat, *The Return*, is because it deals with manhood lost and then found. I also believe it holds the secrets to the blueprint of the restoration of a man's heart to the original design and relationship Jesus enjoyed with the Father. In the steps of the lost son's return home, Jesus shared the keys to finding the path to a restoration of distinctive and authentic manhood. In discovering this I have seen men become better husbands, fathers, sons, and brothers, ultimately better men!

My hope is that when I get through teaching you this story in the way God has shown me through my spiritual father and pastor, Mike Hayes, you will have a deeper understanding of the Father's love and compassion and that it will build a lasting foundation for your faith and purpose as a beloved son of God. For understanding sake, I will unpack this story by presenting again one portion of the story at a time.

Sonship and Fatherhood

"A man had two sons. The younger son told his father, 'I want my share of your estate now before you die.' So, his

father agreed to divide his wealth between his sons" (Luke 15:11-12 NIV).

This is a story about sonship and fatherhood and impatience with the father's timing, but more on that later. Let's talk about the son and father relationship. It's a story best told by Jesus because no one understands sonship more clearly than Jesus, and no one has been fathered better than Jesus, for he was fathered by God himself through Joseph, who was a good man but died early in his life. When Jesus enters his ministry, Joseph is gone. Joseph, to our knowledge, had never seen Jesus perform one miracle. This reality of the absent father is a story repeated by thousands of men in the world. Fatherlessness is a growing epidemic, and in my opinion, is the single greatest loss to men who want to discover true manhood. Satan created this void for a reason, so he could damage the image of manhood and womanhood who by their very creation are supposed to reflect the glory of God on this earth.

In 1900, psychoanalyst Ann Freud, Sigmund Freud's daughter, wrote, "The loss of one's father is the single greatest loss a person can experience." I agree. Other studies on child development suggest that children who did not have fathers at home or who had a father at home but did not have an intimate relationship with him support the idea that dysfunctional fathers raise dysfunctional children. Youth who have an affectionate, caring and loving father tend to be dramatically different. This was especially true for girls whose fathers demonstrated positive qualities when they were little. Thus, when they became women, they were far less promiscuous, compared to women whose fathers fell short of a sound fatherhood pursuit. In 1999, the National Center for Fathering did a poll, "Fathering in America." The poll revealed that 72 percent of the U.S. population believes that fatherlessness is the most significant family or social problem facing America. Recent statistics from 2013 show that:

Sixty-five percent of youth suicides occur in fatherless homes. Ninety percent of homeless and runaway children are from fatherless homes. Eighty-five percent of children with behavioral disorders come from fatherless homes. Eighty percent of rapists come from fatherless homes. Seventy-one percent of high school drop-outs come from fatherless homes. Seventy-five percent of adolescents in chemical abuse centers come from fatherless homes. Seventy percent of juveniles in state-operated institutions come from fatherless homes. Eighty-five percent of youth in prisons grew up in fatherless homes.

Boys and girls without fathers or other significant male role models in their lives are twice as likely to drop out of high school, twice as likely to end up in jail, and four times more likely to need help for emotional or behavioral problems.

The United States is the world's leader in fatherless families. Of the 64 million fathers recorded in the last census, only 41 percent are part of married-couple families with their own children. Each night, some 24 million children (approximately 34 percent of all children) will go to bed in a home where their father does not reside.

These statistical facts strongly support the fact that social dysfunction starts at home with fathers and sons. I have often said this: "Only true masculinity can bestow true masculinity." The same goes for womanhood. I raised three girls that today are godly women. I could show them how to love and serve God. I could show them how a man loves his wife and how a man protects, provides, and cares for his family. But I could not bestow femininity on them; only their mother could do that. Just as this is true for little girls, it is also true for little boys. They don't learn their masculine identity by looking in the mirror or by their mothers' nurturing; they learn it from their dad. Before they can make sense of life, before they can learn about their strength as men, they learn by watching and imitating us men. According to John Eldredge, author of *Wild at Heart*, every little boy asks this question, "Do I have what it takes?" If we as fathers never help our sons answer that question, they will go to the world for the answer. We must affirm them as men and tell them they are loved and that their value is not based on their I.Q, score or accomplishments on a sports field. Their value is based on no other reason than that they are our sons, and not just our sons, but God the Father's sons. When we help them see God in that light, it changes everything. As fathers or mentors, we need to do our best to be that example to them and get them on the path of distinctive and authentic manhood.

We have all heard the old cliché, "life is a journey," and that journey takes us men on many different paths — some good and some not so good. We navigate the best we can, hoping to find the path of true manhood. We all feel the pull — the stubborn pull that leads us somewhere. Of course, the question is where? Where is the path directing us? Where are the circumstances and challenges taking us? I believe this is one of the questions Jesus desired to answer when he shared the story of "The Lost Son." This young man became lost in the maze of paths that lied to him about what it meant to be a real man. After exhausting every path, he found himself facing humiliation, defeat, and desperation. This was when the road became clear. He would choose the path back home to his father. The story ends with a great celebration of his restoration to what, I believe, is true manhood.

We have all been there, searching and searching for what men, authentic men, do; not this distorted pretense of manhood that the enemy has set up, but distinctive and authentic manhood. Brett McKay, the founder of *The Art of Manliness*, a blog dedicated to uncovering the lost path of manhood, says, "There is much discussion these days about manhood and the future of men. Sometimes I will see people try to stop one of these conversations before it's even begun by saying something like, 'Talking about what it means to be a man is meaningless because the whole idea of manhood is relative. It's different in every culture and has changed throughout time.' There is some truth to that argument, in that the ideals of manhood have indeed varied over the centuries and around the world. But it is quite wrong in the assumption that these ideals have not shared some unvarying commonalities. Manhood has always meant something, and though it may come as a surprise to some, it has always meant pretty much the same thing to nearly every society in the world."

I couldn't agree more, and that is why this story is so essential to teach us about what true manhood is like. The story, as I stated earlier, is about two sons, the older, seemingly a hardened religious type, proud, and condemnatory, and the younger one, impatient, reckless, and broken. But keeping to the central part of the story, we will focus most of our attention on the younger son and mention the oldest son's dysfunctional manhood traits at the end.

Impatience with the Father's Timing

"The younger son told his father, 'I want my share of your estate now before you die.' So, his father agreed to divide his wealth between his sons. A few days later this younger son packed all his belongings and moved to a distant land, and there he wasted all his money in wild living" (Luke 15:12-13 NIV).

"It's my money, and I need it now" is from a popular *J.G. Wentworth* commercial that became a mantra of my generation. As we can see from this story, it wasn't anything new.

Asking for his inheritance was not a sin in itself. The sin was in the timing of when he asked for it. The sin was impatience — impatience with the father's timing. The father had an inheritance for him, but it was for an appointed time and an appointed purpose. It was not to be wasted immaturely and prematurely. Still too young and inexperienced, the son needed to stay under his father's covering. He was not ready, but his impatience caused him to prematurely ask for his inheritance now instead of later. To want something now that is designed for later began his downfall and is still a downfall for many men today. The "I want it now" attitude is killing us! As a men's pastor for two decades, I have seen first-hand what this attitude does. I have observed many men over the years who had great potential, but who lost it all because of this one attitude. Impatience with the Father's timing is one of the first manifestations of a rebellious and prideful heart that leads to many problems. When we want something now that is designed for later, this proves we haven't matured enough to handle it, and we will lose it in the end. We will see this as the story unfolds.

I know this first hand. I, too, in my early twenties became impatient and ran off to California to chase my dream of aspiring to become a professional bodybuilder. I had everything: a beautiful young wife who adored me, friends, family, a good church and a growing gym business. But the lure of fame, fortune, and beautiful women took me out of my cocoon of safety and family and positioned me to lose everything. I found myself, like the young man in this story, 'eating from' and involving myself in things that were outside my desired character and my true destiny. I say, "desired" character because I had none at the time. I had plenty of talent but very little character, if any. Talent may get you there, but only character can keep you there. I say "true destiny" because I believe my destiny was to be a pastor and help men in a profound and life-altering way, not just in developing their physique. Impatience, mixed with pride and lust almost destroyed me. It wasn't until I came to my senses and cried out to God for help one night on Venice Beach that my... restoration began.

Wasted Resources

"About the time his money ran out, a great famine swept over the land, and he began to starve. He persuaded a local farmer to hire him, and the man sent him into his fields to feed the pigs. The young man became so hungry that even the pods he was feeding the pigs looked good to him. But no one gave him anything."

So, he says, "Give me my portion now," and packs his stuff up and takes off to the big city to sow his wild oats and there wasted his substance and lost everything. Then, in desperation, joins himself to strangers and begins to work on a pig farm. One day he finds himself so hungry he begins to crave the pig slop, but the owners wouldn't even give him that. It amazes me how, when we are out of the will of God, we compromise our standard of living and begin to crave the nastiest things. I have seen men leave beautiful wives, children, and careers for trampy women. Men lose great jobs or companies for sex, drugs, alcohol, gambling–winding up on the streets eating out of trash cans. The Jewish culture considered pigs the lowest of God's creation. Not only would they not eat the meat of pigs, but they also would not dare touch them. Yet, this boy is working with and feeding pigs and wants to eat what they eat. This is a picture of how far we will go when we lose our way. This is a picture of life without a relationship with the Father.

But then something happened to the boy that made him a man! He got a revelation! Some may call it an epiphany, but it's more than that. It is what I call a righteous convergence of truth! This is what happened to me on that beach. There, I came to myself and caught a whiff of my depravity and didn't like what I smelled. I think it's good to get a nostril full of the pig pen of our sin, for it leads to a repentant heart, which will lead to the restoration of manhood.

God Make Me

"When he came to his senses, he said, 'How many of my father's hired servants have food to spare, and here I am starving to death! I will set out and go back to my father and say to him: Father, I have sinned against heaven and against you. I am no longer worthy to be called your son; make me like one of your hired servants" (Luke 15:17-19 NIV).

"Conation" is among the least used words in the English language. Conation is the part of the mental faculty that has to do with desire, choosing, or resolving. It's the energy of the mind which produces an effort to change. What happened to this boy and me was a conatus moment, but with a twist. Truth began to converge upon him to expel the lies.

In our men's ministry, we often say, "If a lie holds you captive, then only truth can set you free." We all need to come to this place in our lives — where the lie is exposed, and truth from God's Word replaces it. Where we say, "Enough is enough," and ask God to "Change me and make me the man I need to be!" I find it interesting that the son in this story starts off saying, "Give me!" and ends up saying, "Make me!" We all need to get to the point where we get a good whiff of our own cesspool and we say, "This stinks; I stink," and make a change. This is what happened to me. My whole life was about trying to make me. So, I took advantage of everything and everyone to get what I needed to make me. I chased money, muscles and women to make me. It was always about making me. I think one of the most arrogant things a man can say is, "I'm a self-made man." What! You can't even breathe without God! There is no such thing as a self-made man, but I believed the lie and it wasn't until truth converged on me through the life and love of Christ that I started to come to my senses and change my ways.

In the story, the young man comes to his senses and says, "My father's servants live better than this. Here I am living on the street, feeding pigs and starving to death and my father is wealthy, and his servants live and eat better than I do."

This young man, in his moment of truth, in his moment of brokenness, says, "I'm not worthy to be called your son; make me like one of your hired servants." Remember who tells this story? What is it Jesus wants us to catch? Could it be that many times our sense of worth is derived from our failures and lack of performance? Or could it be that we feel unworthy based on our experience with the world, or worse, religion? Are we ever worthy? The night of my convergence of truth when I reached the broken point, I said to God the Father, "Make me. Use me. I don't want to be a champion for this bodybuilding world, I want to be a champion for you." I was there; right where that young man was, coming to my senses. Saying "Make me, make me!" That changed everything. When I got back home, I went to church as soon as I could and went up to the youth pastor who I'd briefly met years earlier and said, "I don't have much to offer, I don't know much of the

Bible, but what I have I offer it to you. Use me wherever you need me; I'm here to serve."

This young man in the story had the same change of heart. He would rather be a servant in his father's house than continue to live the way he was living. This kind of humility was appropriate, but his father had other plans. It reminds me of what Jeremiah the prophet said. "For I know the plans I have for you,' declares the LORD, *'plans to prosper you* and not to harm *you, plans* to give *you* hope and a future" (Jeremiah 29:11 NIV).

The son is willing to relinquish his sonship for servanthood. The condition in which he finds himself helps him long for servant status in his father's house. It is equally interesting that his father does not even respond to his request and quickly begins to restore him. Instant forgiveness, instant restoration, instant recognition. Something he could not do for himself — only his father could. There are things only The Father can do.

Five steps led to this young man's restoration of manhood. These are the same five steps that helped me and help thousands of men to restore their manhood and their heart to the Father in our men's retreats.

1. The Embrace

"So, he returned home to his father. And while he was still a long way off, his father saw him coming. Filled with love and compassion, he ran to his son, embraced him, and kissed him..." (Luke 15:20 NIV).

Do you see what I see? While the son is still a long way off, the father, full of love and compassion, runs to him and kisses him and embraces him! It's important to notice this all happens while he is still on the road. He hasn't even reached the house and showered or put on a change of clothing. He still stinks like pigs, yet his father runs to him and embraces and kisses him!

Runaway

As a kid, I ran away from home. I packed all my belongings in a knapsack, tied it to a stick, grabbed my pellet gun, and headed out the door—but not before I left an audio recording to my mom about why I was leaving. You see, I had four older siblings who were all very smart and successful. I, on the other hand, struggled with school and saw no future. I felt broken, defective, and burdensome to my family. So, in my young mind, I intended to join a circus or become a safari hunter in Africa. I didn't get too far before I became hungry, cold, and scared. I ended up at home that night before dinner, and my mother hugged me at the door, dirty and stinky as I was. It didn't matter to her; she was glad to have me home. I realized she had not found the audio tape I recorded earlier, so I hid it. Years later, my older brother found it and teased me for years until I destroyed it. You don't keep evidence like that around with an older brother like mine. When it comes to perfection; when it comes to the will of God; when it comes to all we are called to be or want to be; we are still a long way off. We can't even come close to approaching God's holiness and perfection, yet we succumb to the pressure of trying to be what we cannot be. Without Him, we spin our wheels and waste our possessions. It's a trap; a trick! The worst part is we are the ones who put these expectations on ourselves, not God. He doesn't place unreasonable expectations on us. People do; parents do; siblings, coaches or teachers do, but not God. Trying to be what we cannot be without the Father is insanity. The father's embrace in this story tells us a lot about the Father in heaven.

He knows what we have done!

He knows where we have been!

He knows when we did it!

Yet He still embraces us as sons whom He loves!

The embrace of restoration began the work of restoration. It is the father's embrace of a son who felt unworthy that makes this story so amazing.

Unworthiness

When I was in Uganda, Africa with a group of pastors, they asked me to preach in a small village church. While there, the Ugandan pastor asked if we would pray for a sick woman in the village after the service. We did not know she had developed AIDS and her body was covered with sores. I had never seen AIDS close up, and the sight broke my heart. As we approached this young woman, she got up off her straw mat and tried to straighten her dress out to be more presentable to us. She wouldn't even look at us because of shame and the feeling of unworthiness, which brought tears to our eyes. The compassion of the Father overwhelmed us, and we laid hands on her and embraced her. This startled her because she expected us to fear her disease, but pure love came over us, and we didn't care. Years later, we heard she was healed. That's our Father! He is good! He is worthy in our unworthiness!

Our restoration always begins with the Father embracing us while we are feeling unworthy. While we still smell of our depravity, He embraces us. In our story, the young son's reaction is not unique or unusual. Most people feel unworthy when they approach God because we know ourselves and our shortcomings. What's so unusual and special about this story that Jesus shared is the father's embrace and the son's reaction. When the son sees his father, he starts to voice his repentance, but the father hugs him and kisses him all the more, showering him with love in front of the whole community. Let me stop here and say that a big part of restoration is the ability to be quick to repent. You shouldn't have to sink to the lowest depths before you repent. Be a quick repenter! I teach at my men's retreats that one of the measures of a man's maturity is how fast he repents. If you must think about it for a long period of time, or have it dragged out of you and exposed, or you must get caught before you repent, then something is wrong. Forgiveness is the same way. If you must dwell on it and hold a grudge for a time, you're not walking in maturity as a man. Let me tell you how fast Jesus forgave — while it happened!

Confession Box

I had repented many times before, but never genuinely. As a Catholic-raised boy, confession to me was
part of the deal. Every year I went to confession where
I sat in a booth-like room with two seats divided by a
wall with a small veiled window. It was known by my
friends as the "confession box." The father (a priest)
would sit on one side, and I would sit on the other.
He asked me what sins I had committed from which
I needed to repent. I would go down the list which
was censored because my mother was sitting in the
church waiting for me and if I had spent a lot of time in
there and in praying the rosary afterwards she'd know
it was bad and would begin asking questions. Plus,
talk about scary, I'm in these dark close quarters with
a total stranger sharing my deepest darkest sins. But
all it meant to me was clearing my plate to start over.
It was not sincere. The night on the beach, however,
was sincere, with snot, tears and a contrite heart. The
difference between feeling sorry and true repentance
is responsibility afterwards. I took full responsibility
for my actions, I quit the blame game. The moment I
did that, my restoration of genuine manhood began.
Today I teach men that the difference between a male

and a man is responsibility. Maturity is not based on age but responsibility.

2. The Robe

"But his father said to the servants, 'Quick! Bring the finest robe in the house and put it on him..." (Luke 15:21NIV).

The father asks for not just any robe, but the finest robe in the house, which represents right-standing, covering, and favor. Notice what the father did not do. He does not tell him to clean up first; he doesn't spray him with cologne. He just removes the ragged, smelly robe from his past and covers him with the robe of right-standing. A "religious spirit" would have said, "Clean up your act first and then we can talk about right-standing." But not this father. He says, "Turn my way and look at me, and I will come running to cover you!" We do not have to get clean and then come to God; we simply come to God, and He gets us clean. For years I thought I had to "get all my ducks in a row" before God could ever use me. I think part of that thinking originated because of the way I experienced church as a kid.

Captain Altar Boy

As I said, I was raised Catholic and attended church every Sunday with my mother. When I came of age, I became an altar boy. Now, for some of you who were not raised Catholic, that is a boy who helps the priest with the church service called a Mass. Both of my older brothers were altar boys, so it was very important that I became one. It is one of the proudest things a Catholic mom can feel for her sons. The only problem with me, I was a little ADD. I was easily distracted and would mess up a lot. For instance, at the beginning of each Mass, the priest would open up the service with a reading of the scripture. My job was to walk in front of him and open a huge Bible, lean it against my chest, and become a human pulpit. There was one problem! I had it upside down, and you couldn't miss it when, to my embarrassment, the priest shook his head and grabbed this huge Bible to turn it right side up. Another time I was to ring what I called the "holy bell" during his recitation of the Lord's Supper. This part was normally reserved for captain altar boy (the oldest) whom I aspired to be someday. Well, that moment came when he called in sick and I was given the task. The only problem was, I couldn't remember what moment in the recitation to do it, so I just rang it a lot until he told me to stop, which was often. There went my chances at captain altar boy.

Dropping Jesus

My worst experience in Mass was during the celebration of the Eucharist, which is communion, when I dropped the host, a small round wafer of bread, blessed by the priest and, according to Catholic theology, transformed into the Lord's literal body. When I dropped it on the floor, I panicked and hid it under my foot, so the priest would not see it. I began praying God would not strike me dead for dropping Jesus and then stepping on Him, only to then lie to the priest that I didn't know what happened to it. I still think I'm paying for that one. An interesting thing happened though; the priest was able to reach down in the chalice (a cup for the wine of the Eucharist or Mass) and find another piece of Jesus to give away. I learned something that day, that even when we feel like we dropped Jesus, when we feel we have made the biggest mistake of our lives... When we feel like we've failed in everything we hold dear: our faith, our belief, our walk, our Jesus— there is always more of Jesus to go around.

Years later at a Catholic summer camp, they talked to us about consideration to joining the priesthood. With my past altar boy experiences, I thought, "That will never happen. First, I stink at it, and secondly, I like girls." But here I am today, not a priest but a pastor. How funny is that? Now, it wasn't that easy because, like the young man in this story, I struggled with the stink of worthlessness and unworthiness. How could I ever be used by God? I ran from my true calling for years, letting the religious demons beat me up with my mistakes and past sins. It wasn't until I received the embrace of the Father's love on that beach in California and His robe of righteousness in Christ that I began to walk in my purpose and calling.

3. The Ring

"Get a ring for his finger..." (Luke 15:22 NIV).

We have to understand this was not just the father putting some bling on his son. This was a full endowment of authority, legitimacy, and identity. A signet ring in that era was how business was transacted. It was a signature and the identity of one's family. Can you imagine the thoughts on religious minds, "Why are you giving this pitiful example of a son your authority and legitimizing his status as your son?" Which brings up a big question—when are we truly redeemed? Is it when we have done everything right? Is it when we have memorized enough scriptures? Is it when we have been saved for a long time? Or is it when our Father slips on our finger the signet ring of His authority and indicates His acceptance of us through Christ Jesus, giving us the authority to sign on the dotted line on His behalf? Why do I say this? Because false religion is an endless struggle for acceptance and worthiness. All we have to do is understand that it is Christ who makes us worthy. Worthiness is never attained by humans but by Christ and Christ alone.

I never felt I measured up to my earthly father's expectations and never heard him say he was proud of me. That came much later–in my forties. It affected my relationship with my heavenly Father. We seem to always project our experiences with our earthly father to those with our heavenly Father, but He's not the same. As we see in this story that Jesus shared, our heavenly Father loves us the same on our worst day. It's not based on performance.

4. The Sandals

"...and sandals for his feet" (Luke 15:22 NIV).

In life there is nothing more basic than shoes. We take it for granted how blessed we are not to have just one pair of shoes but several pairs. By giving his son shoes, this father demonstrates that he cares for his son's future. Our feet carry us, so by giving him shoes, he endows him with the provision, direction, and a sense of destiny he needs. Our destiny is closely related to our vision, which needs provision to accomplish. Money always follows a vision, not the other way around. Some of us here may struggle with provision because we are experiencing "di-vision" with the Lord's money. When we don't tithe, we are in division which opens the door to wasteful living and the devourer to have his way. But when we have turned our hearts toward the father's house and are willing to serve the vision of the house with our time, talent, and treasure, then the father is quick to put on the sandals of pro-vision.

The Father will not prosper us if the money draws us further from Him. Wealth for kingdom men must connect to kingdom purpose. The closer you get to your purpose the more resources will be lavished on you. When I began to honor God with my finances and regularly tithed and gave offerings to the poor, and the work of the ministry, God the Father began to prosper me. His sandals became apparent in my life when he began to take me to many nations to spread the gospel.

His robe, signet ring, and sandals will adorn your life in every way. But wait, He's not finished.

5. The Celebration

"Bring the fattened calf and kill it. Let's have a feast and celebrate. For this son of mine was dead and is alive again; he was lost and is found.' So, they began to celebrate" (Luke 15:23-24 NIV).

The fifth aspect of the father's restoration is the spirit of celebration, joy, and honor. How different churches would be all across America if they simply included this one concept—celebrating the homecoming of those who have been lost. Not condemnation, not pointing a bony finger of accusation, not banishing us to fire and brimstone, but genuinely celebrating with love and compassion as the father did in this story. The spirit of celebration is when your father is already preparing a fatted calf for you before you even turn down the street toward the house. Think about that—the father was fattening a calf before the son even came to his senses. Isn't this a different picture than what religion has painted? Religion depicts an angry God who is tired of dealing with us and is not even sure if He's going to give us a second chance. The true picture of the father is what Jesus is telling us here. While we were yet enjoying our sin and eating the pig slop, he prepared us a place of honor and celebration in advance! "But God showed his great love for us by sending Christ to die for us while we were still sinners" (Romans 5:8 NLT). No crawling, no groveling, no shoving your face in the dirt, no "I told you so." Just love and compassion and celebration!

Rudy, our Dog

Growing up, my father used to try to potty train our many Chihuahuas by having their faces smeared in the poop and smacking them in the butt; it didn't work. When Misty and I got the kids their first dog, a Jack Russel named Rudy, I began the potty training my father's way again—it didn't work. I knew he was a smart dog, so I got a book on training dogs. I discovered that putting a bell on the doorknob and ringing it every time I took him out would cause him to associate the bell with needing to go to the bathroom, but the biggest help was celebrating with him by petting him and saying, "good boy" when he did poop outside. Celebration was the key. Today Rudy is still with us. When he needs to go, he goes up to the back door and barks. We never have had a problem with him, but I can't say the same for our dog sitters who ignore his barking.

Celebration was the crowning point of this young man's restoration. I visited a church in Brazil that took this spirit of celebration to heart. Every time someone would give his life to Christ in a service they would have all the people of the church raise signs and banners that said, "We love you. Welcome to the family. You are home now." They would get out of their chairs and hug that person and shake hands and sing and jump for joy! It was a moment of true celebration. It reminded me of the scripture that says, "I tell you that in the same way there is rejoicing in the presence of the angels of God over one repentant sinner" (Luke 15:10 WNT).

This young man never expected this, and neither did I. When I returned home, my mother had prepared my room with the nicest comforts of home and fed me a wonderful home-cooked meal. She bought me clothes and helped me get back on my feet. At the gym everyone was excited to see me and so proud of what I had accomplished in the sport of bodybuilding. My church was elated and involved me right away in its activities.

Everywhere I went, they celebrated me. The love and acceptance I received overwhelmed me and caused my heart to heal. That's our Father; He celebrates us!

The Older Brother

"Meanwhile, the older son was in the field. When he came near the house, he heard music and dancing. So, he called one of the servants and asked him what was going on. 'Your brother has come,' he replied, 'and your father has killed the fattened calf because he has him back safe and sound.' The older brother became angry and refused to go in. So, his father went out and pleaded with him. But he answered his father, 'Look! All these years I've been slaving for you and never disobeyed your orders. Yet you never gave me even a young goat so I could celebrate with my friends. But when this son of yours who has squandered your property with prostitutes comes home, you kill the fattened calf for him!" (Luke 15:25-30 NIV).

Jesus ends this beautiful story with a bit of a downer. We glimpse the older brother's dysfunctional way of understanding things. The brother has no compassion, no joy or gratitude for the safe return of his little brother. This jealous, unforgiving, critical brother is an example of bitterness and anger. Instead of lovingly receiving his brother who returned home, he became a clear example of what brothers should not do.

The minute he heard that his little brother had left, or heard about his trouble, he should have begun looking for him. He should have been walking with him on the road when his dad saw him. Instead, he pulled a jealous, uncompassionate, accusatory and mean-spirited attitude. As far as we know, he never enters the house to celebrate his brother's homecoming.

When men decide to answer the call of God and surrender to His will and purpose, we will face criticism. We will be judged, we will be ridiculed, and we will be reminded of our past faults. However, we must keep our focus on our future with God rather than on our past with Satan. We cannot allow other people's mean-spirited indictments to pull us off course. If the repentant brother had to face and deal only with his jealous brother, he would never have been received back home.

Years ago, when I first started in ministry, I performed with a strength team called "Strike Force." We would do feats of strength to draw crowds of young people and share our testimony. We did school assemblies in the morning and church evangelism events in the evening. Thousands of young people around the world gave their lives to Christ through these campaigns. It was wonderful.

One day while in a Bible-belt town doing one of our events, we stopped at a supermarket to buy some snacks before we went to the gym. We were wearing our workout clothes, which consisted of colorful baggy pants and tank tops. While standing in the cashier's line, an older snooty, pickle-juice-dipped woman, dressed in a long black and grey dress, looked me up and down and scoffed at our leader and me. She asked us what we did; we told her we were preachers who win people to Christ, to which she replied, "Huh, preachers! What kind of preacher wears that? You would do better if you wore proper clothing."

Well, our leader, not one to let a so-called religious spirit go unchallenged, let her have a mouthful. The lady got a good dose of terms like whitewashed tombs, snakes, vipers, and Pharisee-type stuff. This religious woman judged us by what we wore and not by our hearts—hearts that were totally in love with God and doing His work all around the world with all our might.

Another time an older man rebuked me after an

event where hundreds of young people responded to the gospel. He said he didn't like the fleshly way I presented the gospel because I used strength feats as a vehicle to draw the lost. I asked how he presented the gospel to the lost and if he won many young people to the Lord, and he couldn't answer me. That's when I said, "I like the way I'm doing it better than the way you're not!"

I believe it is clear that the older brother, like the people I just described, portrayed a religious, self-righteous attitude. He would have made the younger son crawl. This type of religion does that. It would have portrayed the father sitting in the house with a scowl on his face only to send a servant to meet the younger son with soap and water and make him sleep in the servant's ranch house for a while before he even spoke to him. This type of religion would have said, "You're not even worthy of servanthood in this house." This reflected the older son's attitude; he was the picture of a mean religious spirit. Not only would he not embrace him or celebrate that he had now safely arrived home, but he was the first to bring up his faults and past sins. Notice the father never brought it up, but the older son did. But we are not dealing with this type of religion here; we are dealing with Jesus who was all about relational religion, loving religion, forgiving religion, and Jesus points it out. This made the Pharisees and Sadducees, the false religious men of the day, unsettled and angry because they knew they represented the older son in the story. Now, of course, when I say false religion, I'm talking about the kind that is self-righteous, judgmental and mean-spirited like the older brother. This is why at my men's retreats I always end by asking the men to circle up, look each other in the eyes, and say, "You are my brother, you are not alone. I will not let you leave home and eat pig slop. I will come and get you. They will have to come through me to get to you. This is my commitment as your brother." I also have them hold stones and drop them in front of the other brothers and say, "No stones here, my brother, just love, acceptance, and grace."

3

The Hero Inside

"Manhood is the social barrier that societies must erect against entropy, human enemies, the forces of nature, time, and all the human weaknesses that endanger the tribe's life. It is the need for true heroes."

– David D. Gilmore

"How long will you gad about, O you backsliding daughter? For the LORD has created a new thing in the earth – a woman shall encompass a man (hero)"

(Jeremiah 31:22 NKJV).

I believe inside every man there is an innate desire for hero status. People desire to see heroes, to be heroes. This is why they will stand in long lines to shake their hands or to get autographs. Genuine heroes are inspirational examples to emulate because they are strong, noble and selfless. What man worth his salt wouldn't want that? At least I did.

Bodybuilding

The only problem is the fact that I was not in the right company of true manly heroes who could model it for me. See, my story begins with me growing up in a Brazilian immigrant family in the suburbs of New Orleans, Louisiana. As a self-educated man, my father worked most of his life as a longshoreman on shipping docks. Before that, he was a seaman who came to America as a merchant marine. So, you can imagine the type of men my father was around. Not what you would call great role models of manhood. Most were convicts, connivers, gamblers, hard drinkers, brawlers, and womanizers. Much of this he brought home and passed on to his children. I was the youngest of five. As a child, I developed severe ear infections that caused a speech impediment and, as a result, missed much of my foundational schooling. Coupled with a learning disability and parents who had very little education and no idea how to help me, it became the cause of great frustration in my life, not to mention embarrassment.

Earlier on I became a fighter, scrapping my way up the pecking order in my neighborhood. Promiscuity, deception, and theft characterized the way of life in my neighborhood. Fortunately, we lived far enough from the city that I never entered into a gang lifestyle and had enough athletic ability to keep me out of any real trouble. My love for adventure and outdoors kept me safe as well. My desire to be a hero led me to join the police force and later to enter the sport of bodybuilding.

At age thirteen a friend showed me a picture of Arnold Schwarzenegger, and I was hooked. He looked like what I imagined a hero would look like, and I determined to use bodybuilding as my scaffolding for heroism. Within a few short years, I had built a nationally competitive physique, winning everything locally I could travel to. In 1983 I flew to California for the first time and won the Teenage Nationals, and then in 1986 I competed in the Mr. USA and placed second in my class as one of the youngest in the competition. That showing catapulted me onto the international scene.

That same year I got married to my long-term girlfriend, got a manager/promoter, and moved to Venice, California, known as the mecca of bodybuilding at the time. Venice became the launching pad of my brief but extremely successful career. Within just eight months I appeared on the covers of the greatest bodybuilding magazines in the world. The fanfare and attention overwhelmed me. I was not ready for it. My character did not match the quality of my physique, and my father's ways came crashing in. Promiscuity, deception, and violence took over. It caused the demise of my young marriage. At first, I just thought it would blow over, and I would get my stuff together and save my marriage, but that never happened. Instead, it got worse, and my search for the hero within and without never came. I met many who the world thought were heroes. Heck, I even thought they were, but I soon discovered that they were not much different from what I saw at home. I continued to climb the ladder of bodybuilding stardom, more magazine covers, commercials, small parts in movies, and I grew a successful personal training business that kept me busy. But none of it fulfilled me, and it definitely did not transform me into the hero for which I'd hoped. One night while walking Venice Beach in desperation for answers for my broken heart and the crushing shame of the weak man I had become, I cried out to God in a way that I had never done in the past. There on that beach, I discovered that though I grew up in a religious system that created a good image of a God, I had not known Him as a Father. I needed a Father and that night I cried out

"Abba Father" for the first time, which is what Jesus called the Father, "Papa" in Aramaic. That moment I went from a religion to a real relationship and a hero began to immerge. There on that beach, I met the man I wanted to emulate, the hero that called from deep within my soul. That night everything changed for me. I made Christ my Lord and Savior and gave Him my all. I became hungrier for God's purpose than I did for the career of bodybuilding. I felt a calling I didn't even know existed.

Soon after, I packed up my belongings and returned home to Louisiana and joined the church where I first responded to the gospel years before. There I connected with a youth pastor named Mitch Chappetta, and he began to mentor me. Later, I was introduced to Ed Cole, a powerful teacher, author, and founder of C.M.N. (Christian Men's Network). Through his manhood teachings and our personal relationship, I began to learn the way of "distinctive and authentic manhood" according to God's Word. I never forgot the honor of speaking at one of his events and years later introducing him at my own church men's conference. As he walked up to the pulpit, now weak with age, he paused, threw his arms around me and said, "You're my hero!" That moment defined itself as one of the greatest moments of my life. Of course, I argued that *he* was *my* hero, but he would have nothing of the sort.

To date, I have preached the gospel in twenty plus nations. I have seen tens of thousands come to Christ. But my greatest passion is my monthly men's retreats called *The Return, Heroes Return* and *The Awakening.* These events are comprised of several days of God-seeking, self-searching, and spiritual training designed uniquely for molding men into the model that Christ provided. I give them godly anchors to fasten their manhood to. Thousands have gone through it, and it has taken off internationally. People say it is my wheelhouse, my lane, and God has uniquely gifted me for it. I don't know about all that, but what I do know is that I'm passionate about it, and I love the environment it creates for men—an environment where they experience true freedom and where they can become the kind of heroes to which God has called them.

The Making of a Hero

So, how do we encompass this hero in us? I'm glad you asked that question. The root word for *"man"* in Jeremiah 31:22 is the Hebrew word *"gabar."* It describes a man of strength, bravery, and valor. It carries the idea of a warrior hero type, a champion, a mighty man of valor, as in the story of Gideon in Judges 6:12. The same word is used in Isaiah 9:6 for "Mighty God" about the Messiah. The word *"Mighty"* has the additional meaning of "hero." The Lord is the "Infinite Hero" of His people, the "Divine Warrior" who has triumphed over sin and death.

The *"backsliding daughter"* in Jeremiah 31:22 is Israel. She (Israel) has been unfaithful, but in the future, she will seek out her God and ask to be united with Him, and He will restore her. But He warns Israel that it will be in a very unusual way. Israel, born to be a great nation, a heroic nation, finds itself captured by their enemy, the Babylonians, because of their refusal to obey God. In this chapter, God encourages Israel that He won't forget them, that there is hope and that future generations will return to Israel and restore her to her former glory. God's choice of restoration is so remarkable it's likened to God recreating a new thing. Notice the scripture says, *"a woman encompassing a man (hero)."* This is probably the most difficult verse to understand in the Book of Jeremiah. One possible idea is that a woman will seek, or court, a man. Here is why that is so unusual. In that culture, a woman would not normally court a man, so this would truly indicate something unusual. Secondly, it could refer to Mary encompassing Jesus (our ultimate hero) as his mother. Another thought is that it represented an expression of its day whose meaning got lost over time. Whatever it is, one thing is for sure; it speaks of an unusual path that God chooses to encompass the making of a hero.

Zeroes to Heroes

If you noticed, God would use the most peculiar people to transform into heroes. King David was one of them. When we are first introduced to David, he is a little pimple-faced kid, who his father didn't think enough of to invite him to the kingly anointing of Samuel the prophet.

> "So, Samuel did what the LORD said, and went to Bethlehem. And the elders of the town trembled at his coming, and said, 'Do you come peaceably?' And he said, 'Peaceably; I have come to sacrifice to the LORD. Sanctify yourselves, and come with me to the sacrifice.' Then he consecrated Jesse and his sons, and invited them to the sacrifice. So, it was, when they came, that he looked at Eliab and said, 'Surely the LORD'S anointed is before Him.' But the LORD said to Samuel, 'Do not

look at his appearance or at the height of his stature, because I have refused him. For the Lord does not see as man sees; for man looks at the outward appearance, but the LORD looks at the heart.' So, Jesse called Abinadab and made him pass before Samuel. And he said, 'Neither has the LORD chosen this one.' Then Jesse made Shammah pass by. And he said, 'Neither has the LORD chosen this one.' Thus, Jesse made seven of his sons pass before Samuel. And Samuel said to Jesse, 'The LORD has not chosen these.' And Samuel said to Jesse, 'Are all the young men here?' Then he said, 'There remains yet the youngest, and there he is, keeping the sheep.' And Samuel said to Jesse, 'Send and bring him. For we will not sit down till he comes here.' So he sent and brought him in. Now he was ruddy, with bright eyes, and good-looking. And the LORD said, 'Arise, anoint him; for this is the one!' Then Samuel took the horn of oil and anointed him in the midst of his brothers, and the Spirit of the LORD came upon David from that day forward. So Samuel arose and went to Ramah" (1 Samuel 16:4-13 NKJV).

We see this pattern throughout scripture: Moses, Gideon, Jephthah and the list goes on. But the story of

David is my favorite because it is so unusual and serves as a great example of what encompasses heroism. In the next chapters, we will learn what transformed David's life, and others around him, from zeroes to heroes.

Lion-Like Faces

"Some Gadites joined David at the stronghold in the wilderness, mighty men of valor, men trained for battle, who could handle shield and spear, whose faces were like the faces of lions, and were as swift as gazelles on the mountains" (1 Chronicles 12:8 NKJV).

This tribe of men, described as men with lion-like faces is a mighty visual picture of courage. They went on to form the famed "mighty men of David" in the Bible. These were valiant men, men trained for battle! Their feats of war were legendary. One killed 800 men in a single battle by himself; another fought so courageously to defend a bean field for David that they had to peel the sword out of his hand because the muscles in his hands locked up. Another decided to chase a lion on a snowy day into a pit and kill it, with nothing but a club, and for no apparent reason except that he could! These are the type of men I want to hang out with, don't you? Well, you can. The church is meant to be a gathering place for men like this, but the enemy has caused it to be a place of lying faces. These are men who smile and say that all is well when it's not. I know because I was one of those men and, being a men's pastor today, I see it all the time. At our intensives we work hard to change that. We replace lies with truth and men become free to be lions again. The Andrizo tribe, as we call them, are such men. They are men who have slain pride and walked in humility, honesty, and the Holy Spirit and because of that, they have lion-like faces!

We need courageous lion-faced men again. Men, this is important because we are living in challenging times. There is more pressure to conform to a worldly man's perspective than at any other time in history. Men are bombarded from every side, and it's going to take courageous lion-faced men to stand up and fight for righteousness. I believe that we are on the spiritual brink of the greatest revival of all time! I believe that we are going to see a harvest of souls as we have never seen in the history of mankind. I believe that God is raising up groups of lion-faced men that will be strong and courageous, and will finally conquer the land for God. These are men that will grab hold of the promises of God and take possession of the land and fulfill the purposes of God for their lives. Acts 13:36 says, "... *and David served the purpose of God in his own generation... and fell asleep and was buried with his fathers...*" I don't know about you, but I want to finish like that, serving the purpose of God in my generation. To do this, we as men must be willing to lay down our lives for the success of a future generation, and this is going to take courageous lion-faced men!

A Passionate and Anointed Environment

Webster's Dictionary describes passion as a "burning intensity or desire." I like to describe it as, "the degree of difficulty or pain one is willing to endure to attain one's goal." The men around David were mighty men who proved their valor in battle. They endured tremendous difficulty in life, from the harsh wilderness conditions to the many attacks of the enemy. They were men who trained for war, who could handle their weapons skillfully. This doesn't come without discipline, determination, and passion.

Savage Sets

When I was a competitive bodybuilder, a well-known bodybuilding author, Robert Kennedy, wrote a book called "Savage Sets" about hard core workouts and iron warriors of the gym. I was chosen for the cover. As a competitive bodybuilder, going to the gym was not an option but a passion that drove me through insane workouts. I would show up at the gym at six in the morning with two training partners I affectionately called the "Titans." One of the definitions for "Titans" includes men of overwhelming size and strength. This fit them perfectly. We would come in and turn the music up loud (I managed the gym) and scream, "Weights, you are our slaves, and we are your masters, you will yield to our power and obey us!" There were times when I bit the Olympic bars to psych myself up before lifting. We would yell and slap each other so hard it would leave bruises on our skin. The passion went through the roof, and if you trained with me, you would soon realize why I was so strong and built the kind of physique I built at a young age. Passion was the key, and a little crazy gene didn't hurt.

Cave Men

In 1 Samuel 22:1-2 David is running for his life, and he ends up in a cave called Adullam. There he gathers a bunch of misfits and outlaws. But then something happens. In the environment of his passion and anointing, these men transformed into some of the greatest warriors that ever lived. What happened? Like produces like; that's what happened. The environment you create produces either an environment for zeroes or heroes. They were Braveheart-type men. What made the difference? A passionate, anointed environment created by David.

Big Boys Club

When I lived in Louisiana, I was the big man in the gym and one of the few to use 150-pound dumbbells. My bench was just under five hundred. But when I moved to Venice, California, I began to work and train at the famed Gold's Gym where the big boys trained, men like Arnold Schwarzenegger and Lou Ferrigno and others. There, for the first time, I saw a 250-pound dumbbell. I thought wow, who lifts that? I found out many did. Within a few months, I was lifting that 250-pound dumbbell and blowing past a 500-pound bench. What made the difference? An environment characterized by bigger, stronger men! As I said earlier, like produces like. Whoever you hang with you will be like. *"Do not be misled: "Bad company corrupts good character*" (1 Corinthians 15:33 NIV).

I was in the big boys club now and I needed to start rising up to the level of strength that the environment required to be the best. The environment strengthens you or weakens you! What environment are you in? Are you the biggest, the strongest and the smartest of your circle? If so, it's time to enlarge your circle and change your environment!

Heroes Produce Heroes

We have a ministry we started called *Heroes Return*. *Heroes Return* originated from a desire to reach our soldiers and first responders who suffer from mental afflictions or soul wounds caused by the trauma of war and disasters. These returning veterans, the sons and daughters of our country, are heroes who have lost their way. Divorce, suicide, PTSD and other sociological disorders are at an all-time high. We discovered the separation they feel, not fitting in, and the lack of "mission" that characterizes many. All this leaves our veterans feeling lost. The effects of physical and emotional injuries they have experienced leave many in the wilderness of pain and confusion not knowing what to do and where to turn. We get them "off the grid," at our ranch and give them purpose again and create a safe environment where truth can replace lies, and they can get restored, healed and made whole. Men find camaraderie and are surrounded by a "squad" of men who serve as "wingmen" to each Hero. What makes it so effective is that the majority of our staff is made up of veterans, officers, firemen and other first responders, who are passionate and anointed for this ministry. We have a saying in our men's ministry, "Free men, free men!" The newest is "Healed heroes, heal heroes!" When these men realize that they are not defective or damaged, they are only different because of their experience, we then channel that experience into making them an instrument of healing to others.

A Touched Heart

"And Saul also went home to Gibeah; and valiant men went with him, whose hearts God had touched" (1 Samuel 10:26 NKJV).

In every generation God raises up heroes to fight for righteousness—to bring a nation that has fallen away back to God. I grew up hearing and reading about these heroes in the church who against all odds did valiant and mighty things for God. As I got older,

I realized how few and far between these heroes were! Several years ago, a movie came out on the big screen called *End of the Spear*. It told the great story of Jim Elliot and his four friends who decided as missionaries to reach out to the Waodani tribe in the Ecuadorian rainforest in the Amazon basin in 1956. Members of that tribe brutally murdered them, but then something amazing happened; the killers were converted by the wives and children of these deceased men. Here were five men who became heroes, who gave the ultimate sacrifice, their own lives for the cause of Christ. My wife and I sat in an empty theater in the middle of the day watching this film. I was awestruck by their sacrifice and devotion to the cause of Christ. I wondered why there were not more people in the audience. My wife quickly reminded me we were viewing this movie in the middle of the day. But I realized that this didn't stop people from seeing *King Kong* next door.

Maybe it's just me, but when great movies like this come out where courage, forgiveness, and sacrifice are captured in such a way, I have to wonder, why don't more people see it? Are we so desensitized in America that we are not moved anymore by true heroes?

Have we become so civilized and tamed in our

faith that we forget more than half the world has not heard the gospel and will not hear it unless more men and women like this rise up? I don't know about you, but I choose to be this kind of man. Not that I want to die as a martyr, but I don't want to live my life thinking about what could have been. I want to actually do it! Jim Elliot penned in his journal, "He is no fool who gives what he cannot keep to gain what he cannot lose." This statement galvanized a whole generation of missionaries who flocked to foreign mission fields. Why? ... because their hearts were touched for a greater purpose than themselves.

A Selfless Act

"Once when David was at the rock near the cave of Adullam, the Philistine army was camped in the valley of Rephaim. The Three (who were among the Thirty – an elite group among David's fighting men) went down to meet him there. David was staying in the stronghold at the time, and a Philistine detachment had occupied the town of Bethlehem. David remarked longingly to his men, 'Oh, how I would love some of that good water from the well by the gate in Bethlehem.' So the Three broke through the

Philistine lines, drew some water from the well by the gate in Bethlehem, and brought it back to David. But David refused to drink it. Instead, he poured it out as an offering to the LORD. 'God forbid that I should drink this!' he exclaimed. 'This water is as precious as the blood of these men who risked their lives to bring it to me.' So David did not drink it. These are examples of the exploits of the Three" (1 Chronicles 11:15-19 NIV).

I love this story; what incredible selflessness. These men love and believe so much in their leader that they risk their lives to bring him a glass of water from his favorite well. David doesn't ask them for it; he is longing out loud. But he's in the company of heroes who love him. He is so touched by their willingness to get in harm's way, just to bless him, that he pours it out to God as a drink offering. But here lies one of the greatest attributes of a hero — sacrifice. "Greater love has no one than this than to lay down one's life for his friends" (John 15:13 NKJV).

There is a great story of a little monk named Telemachus who lived in the fourth century. One day this monk felt God calling him to Rome. So, he placed his possessions in a little satchel, threw the bag over his shoulder, and started out over the dusty, westward road to Rome, the capital of the world. When he got there, people ran about the city in great excitement. He had arrived on a day when the gladiators were to fight in the great coliseum. Everyone had headed to the amphitheater to watch the entertainment. He walked into the amphitheater and sat down among 80,000 people who cheered as the gladiators came out. "This isn't right!" he thought. Telemachus got up out of his seat, ran down the steps, climbed over the wall, walked out to the center of the amphitheater, and stood between two large gladiators. He put his hands up and cried out, "In the name of Christ, stop!" The crowd laughed and jeered. One of the gladiators slapped Telemachus in the stomach with the flat of his sword and sent him spinning off into the dust. Telemachus got up and again stood between the two huge gladiators. More forcefully this time, he shouted, "In the name of Christ, stop!" This time the crowd chanted, "Run him through!" As commanded, one of the gladiators took his sword and ran it through Telemachus' stomach. The monk fell into the dust as the sand ran red. One last time, Telemachus weakly cried out, "In the name of Christ, stop." He died on the amphitheater floor. The crowd grew silent. One by one, they began to leave. Within minutes the amphitheater emptied.

(Theodoret, Bishop of Cyrrhus in Syria (393-457 A.D.) *Ecclesiastical History*)

History records this as the last gladiatorial contest in the history of the Roman Empire. Never again in this stadium did men kill each other for the entertainment of crowds — all because one tiny selfless hero who could hardly be heard above the tumult took a courageous stand.

Heroes do this. They see things in different dimensions. To them, this earthy realm pales to the heavenly realm. Like the Apostle Paul, they push toward the *"upward call of God in Christ Jesus"* (Philippians 3:14).

So, here is my synopsis to becoming a hero. Get around anointed environments of great men who are passionate, whose hearts God has touched and then willingly lay down your life for the cause of Christ. I guarantee a hero will emerge.

Andrizo

"It's hard to describe manliness in isolation — that is, apart from the flesh and blood of men who embody it. It's something that you instinctively recognize and feel when you encounter it in another."

— Brett McKay

"Be alert and on your guard; stand firm in your faith. Act like men and be courageous; grow in strength!"

(1 Corinthians 16:13 NLT).

Now, why do I find it critically important to title this book Andrizo Man? What is the essence of this term Andrizo? Andrizo is a call, an ancient war-cry that awakens men to submit to a higher standard of manhood.

One of my most prolific inspirers of manhood, as I've stated, was the late Ed Cole, who often said, "Manhood and Christ-likeness are synonymous." As such, I will be drawing parallels between the Word of God and Christ-likeness as it pertains to distinctive, authentic manhood.

Wild-Eyed Warrior

I loved to play "Cowboys and Indians" as a kid. On one such occasion, I was on the cowboy side of the game, which was unusual because I was an archer and loved playing the warrior. The clubhouse served as the fort under attack. We tried our best to defend it with our Daisy BB guns, but the casualties were building up. One of the new guys to the game included a boy from another neighborhood who got a little carried away with his role as an Indian. The rules were no shooting BBs, arrows or spears at the face or groin. All other areas were an open game. As the battle continued I heard a loud war cry, the door busted open and a wild-eyed war-painted Indian ran in yelling and flung a spear at me. It hit me in the ear, and it stuck in my skull. I was in shock as blood ran down my neck. The new boy was equally shocked. Now, I don't know about your neighborhood growing up, but in mine, there existed an unspoken rule; when someone got hurt, you ran because no one wanted to be blamed and get in trouble. The new boy obviously knew the same rule and ran. After the initial shock of walking into my house with a spear stuck in my head, my mother rushed me to the hospital where I got several stitches and a cool story. As for the new boy, he never came around again. Smart boy!

Ancient War Cry

I share that funny story about Cowboys and Indians because tucked in the book of First Corinthians, I found an ancient war cry that has become the anthem for manhood in our church and throughout the world. In chapter sixteen verse thirteen is a Greek word used only once by the Apostle Paul that transcends what the world considers manhood. It is the epitome of distinctive and authentic manhood. It is distinctive because maleness is a matter of birth, but manhood is a matter of a distinctive choice! It is authentic because God's version of manhood has been hi-jacked by the enemy and replaced with a counterfeit.

The word is *"Andrizo."* The word Andrizo is one of the most stirring and powerful words in Greek for manhood I have ever discovered. Andrizo is the march to a different beat. It's a higher standard and above and beyond the world's image of manhood.

Its Hebrew twin word *"chazaq"* is also an ancient war cry God has used for thousands of years to awaken men to war and authentic manhood. Chazaq is found over three-hundred times in the Old Testament. It's attached to almost every great warrior of the Bible we know. Caleb is one such individual. Remember him? He was the faithful friend of Joshua who spied out the Promised Land and came back with a positive report announcing they would eat the giants for breakfast. At age eighty he did just that, taking the very mountain the giants lived on. The man's actual name meant "War-like cry." That's Chazaq!

Pastor Eric Ludy describes *Chazaq* as "The rock-like oomph of the spiritually zealous heart; the game face of a mighty man; the flush of spiritual fervor in the veins of a warrior before an attack." You can see why I call it a war cry.

In the Greek Septuagint, everywhere Chazaq is written it's translated Andrizo. We don't have a word like this today, spiritually speaking. We should—because just like in Paul's day, men don't know what they're up against. Many men today don't realize we are at war. They don't understand we are in hostile territory; this is not a time of peace. Erwin McManus in

his book, *The Barbarian Way,* said, "To be born of (
to be made a citizen in the kingdom of God — and
kingdom is at war. We can never confuse the adva
ing kingdom of God with Paradise. Salvation is not
entry into a paradise lost; it is enlistment in the army (
God. The Bible tells us in no uncertain terms that there
is a battle raging. We are called to be warriors of light
in dark places. When we are born again, we are not
dropped into a maternity ward, but we are dropped
into a war zone. When you enter the kingdom of God
there is no safe zone or waiting room. There really isn't
even a boot camp. It's on-the-job, on-the-field training.
You get to take your first steps of a new life in the middle of a battlefield." The war is not against flesh and
blood. The war is not against people. It's against the
devil who puppeteers the men of this age. This battle
is not only for the souls of men but for manhood itself.
Manhood made in the image of God.

Pastor Eric Ludy gives a powerful speech on the
word Chazaq. Here is a short version of it with the
word Chazaq exchanged for Andrizo for the sake of
this teaching. "Men, we are living in the greatest moment in the history of mankind. As men of God, we are
in a position to see men set free from the bondage and

struggles that have held them in chains for decades. Do you realize you have the armory of heaven at your disposal, that you have everything you need for victory, to push back the enemy's forces? So, when we hear the word *Andrizo,* our knuckles, spiritually speaking, should turn white with anticipation of pounding the enemy and taking names! Who had *Andrizo?* David against Goliath had it. A boy ran headlong towards a nine-foot giant with nothing but rocks and a sling. That's *Andrizo! Andrizo* says, "NO! I'm NOT weighing the odds or the impossibilities! This is for my God, and He fights my battles— "I am more than a conqueror!" "I can do all things through Christ who strengths me!" "No weapon formed against me shall prosper!" Who had *Andrizo?* Moses, who stood against the greatest army of his day with nothing, but a staff and a promise had it and said, "Let my people go, or else!" Moses understood *Andrizo.* In his farewell speech to the people before they entered the Promised Land, Moses laid down the ground rules for the kingdom to be established when they crossed the Jordan. Moses turned to the people and said: "Be strong and of good courage (*Andrizo!*), do not fear nor be afraid of them; for the LORD your God, He is the One who goes with you.

He will not leave you nor forsake you." Then Moses called Joshua and said to him in the sight of all Israel, "Be strong and of good courage (*Andrizo!*), for you must go with this people to the land which the LORD has sworn to their fathers to give them, and you shall cause them to inherit it" (Deuteronomy 31:6-7 NKJV). Moses, like Paul, knew that the men they were leading were undefined men who were coming into their own—that they would inherit the promise. He also knew they would enter into hostile territory; thirty-one hostile empires awaited them. One of these empires consisted of all giants, ancestors of Goliath! He wanted to make sure they knew what it took—*Andrizo!* In actuality, Moses is passing the war cry torch of manhood to the next generation, not unlike what Paul did in the New Testament. So, what can happen to the world if Christian men once again "get their war cry on?" We get what the Apostles got after Pentecost! Look at Peter. One moment he's cowering down, denying Christ, and the next moment he is a preaching machine. In one sermon 3,000 were added to the kingdom. What happened to him? The Spirit of the Lord came upon him! The Spirit of THE Lord Sabaoth! The Lord of the armies of Heaven! *Andrizo* came on him, that's what happened. Why do we need a war cry like *Andrizo*? We need it because mere casual Christianity is not going to push back darkness! The kingdom of God suffers violence, and the violent take it by force! It takes redeemed, blood-bought, Spirit-filled, transformed *Andrizo* men! Men, we are here right now, today, we have crossed the Jordan because of Christ, and we are standing on the banks of the Promised Land and God is saying, "Go get it. Go get your inheritance as my men. You will win! Just obey me! Even if you die, you win!"

The Andrizo Gap

This is not to scare you; this is to inspire you. The Bible says, "I looked for a man among them who would build up the wall and stand before me in the gap on behalf of the land, so I would not have to destroy it, but I found none" (Ezekiel 22:30). This scripture clearly tells us God is looking for men today who will stand in the gap of manhood and say, "Here I am!"

When God had enough of Job's whining he said, "Stand up like a man and brace yourself for battle..." (Job 40:7 TLB). God needed Job to Andrizo up! He needed him to, "gird up his loins" as the King James translation says. To gird up your loins meant you were getting ready for action. Back in the Bible days, men wore flowing tunics. Around the tunic, they wore belts. While tunics were comfortable, cool and breezy, the hem of the tunic would often get in the way if a man needed to fight in battle or perform hard labor. So, when men had to fight or had to work hard, they would roll up their sleeves and lift the hem of their tunic and tuck it into their belt or tie it in a knot to keep it off the ground. The effect created a pair of shorts that provided more freedom of movement. Thus, to tell someone to "gird up their loins" was to tell them to get ready for hard work or battle. It was the ancient way of saying "time to man up!" Loins also represented the seat of strength and vigor of a man or the center of pro-creative power as in when Jacob receives his Divine promise that "kings shall come out of his loins" (Genesis 35:11). Loins also depicted truthfulness and faithfulness. As in Ephesians 6:14 "...having girded up thy loins with truth..." In Isaiah 11:5 the Messiah is described: "Righteousness shall be the girdle of his waist, and faithfulness the girdle of his loins." Why is this important? I believe that this is one of the reasons the enemy attacks men in the loin area. I believe the promiscuity and porn epidemic in America today can be traced to the enemy trying to destroy a man's ability in the area of righteousness and faithfulness because he knows if he can keep him bound in shame and guilt he can keep him from standing up for what it right!

Porn War

Did you know that in 2003 the average age of a young man being exposed to porn was eleven? In 2012 the average age was eight and now I hear it is as low as six. Why do you think the enemy is ramping it up? Because we don't have enough Andrizo Men standing in the gap and talking to their sons or brothers about the danger and destruction of porn, because many are addicted themselves. So, what am I trying to say? Men, life is a battle, and the Christian life is the most intense battle of all, but porn is a war we must win. It takes a Andrizo Man to live the Christian life because our enemy is playing for keeps. Men, today more than ever, God is looking for Andrizo Men who are Standup Men who will let God show Himself strong through them! The Apostle Paul was such a man. He was a Standup guy who lived the Andrizo life. The Andrizo life had served him well over the hard years of ministry. In his writings to the church in Corinth, he deals with a group of men who were being taken out left and right by all kinds of vile sexual sins. Not knowing what godly living meant, they had no spiritual war cry like the men of old to unite them to the cause of distinctive and authentic manhood. So, Paul, seeing this, pulls from his roots this ancient war cry *Chazaq* and finds the powerful Greek word *Andrizo*, telling them to *"act like men!"* The only problem was they had no idea what that looked like, so Paul schooled them on the ancient paths of manhood.

Broken Males

To truly understand the path of manhood that Paul is trying to take the men of Corinth down you have to know a little about the city of ancient Corinth. Corinth had a reputation as the most corrupt and perverted city of its time.

Corinth was the fourth largest city of its day. Only Rome, Alexandria and Antioch were larger. Corinth was the main trading route, a melting pot of nationalities, philosophers, and religions and like many port cities it was very prosperous. But with its explosive growth and diversity it was ripe for all sorts of corruption. Idolatry flourished, and there were more than a dozen pagan temples employing at least a thousand prostitutes. Corinth's reputation was such that prostitutes in other cities began to be called "Corinthian girls." It was a cesspool of sexual immorality. With its chief deity "Venus," the goddess of love, or more accurately lust, you can bet Corinth became one of the most perverse, twisted, and broken male cultures of its time. Why even the Romans and Greeks looked down at Corinthian men. Whenever Romans put on one of their plays, they looked for Corinthian men to play the role of brawlers and drunkards. They made Corinthian men the brunt of their dirty jokes. The Greeks even created a verb after them calling it "to Corinthianize," meaning a life of immorality and drunkenness. Think about that, some of the worst paganistic and immoral societies looked down their noses at Corinthian men. Now that tells you something.

Many of the cities to which Paul traveled were rife with immorality and demonic activity. But the city of Corinth took the cake. When he first traversed the long road that led into Corinth, he walked past intricately carved idols that lined the road on each side. These statues—most of which were naked—had been vividly painted, with great attention paid to even the smallest details, to make them appear as vibrant and lifelike as possible. Thus, when Paul walked down on that street into the city of Corinth for the first time, flanked by brightly colored idols on all sides, it was as if he was walking through a corridor of living pornography. Paul, a true "Andrizo Man" boldly entered that city to proclaim the light of truth and built a church in the face of unspeakable darkness. So, you see why he was getting reports of jealousy, immorality, pride and a slew of other problems in this young church. Many believe Apollos was appointed a pastor for this church. Apollos was a great orator but young in the things of Christ and was very busy traveling like Paul. Paul was about two hundred miles away in Ephesus building another church, when he wrote these letters. He realized that the men of the church were confused about how real men act and began a dialogue with them about the virtues it takes to embrace distinctive and authentic manhood because they had no clue. Paul's problem then seemed to be our problem today.

5

Tarnished Image of Manhood

"In an increasingly androgynous society, modern men are confused about their role and what it means to be honorable, courageous and well-rounded men. The causes of this malaise are many — from the cultural to the technological. One factor is simply the lack of direction offered men in the popular culture. Men's magazines today are largely about sex, sports cars and getting six-pack abs."

— Brett McKay

There is a lot of talk about what a real man is these days. Of course, society has its opinion, and we know it is skewed by Satan's demonic ploy to emasculate manhood and pervert its image. He is so good at puppeteering the men of this age that he can deceive one of the greatest male athletes of our times, an Olympic hero, and make him think he is a woman. If you don't think his plan is working just look at how media portrays men. The sit-coms and movies continue to depict men as idiots, racists or sex maniacs, anything but godly men. Even the "good" shows like, "The Cosby Show," are in question because the actor behind the character of Dr. Cliff Huxtable couldn't live up to the clean image he created.

Why does the enemy do this? ...because man was made in God's image, and Satan hates that about us. So, he makes the world laugh at men because, in essence, they are laughing at God! But manhood is not a laughing matter to God. Manhood is not a joke to God. God is serious about our manhood!

Duncan Brannan, a minister friend of mine, shared an Old Testament story with me that strongly makes this point. It's found in Second Samuel.

> *"Later, the king of the Ammonites died, and Hanun his son reigned in his stead. David said, 'I will show kindness to Hanun son of Nahash, as his father did to me.' So David sent his servants to console him for his father's death; and they came into the land of the Ammonites, but the princes of the Ammonites said to Hanun their lord, 'Do you think that it is because David honors your father that he has sent comforters to you? Has he not rather sent his servants to*

*you to search the city, spy it out, and overthrow it?'
So Hanun took David's servants and shaved off half
their beards and cut off their garments in the middle
at their hips and sent them away. When it was told
David, he sent to meet them, for the men were greatly
ashamed. And the king said, 'Tarry at Jericho until
your beards are grown, and then return.' And when
the Ammonites saw that they had made themselves
obnoxious and disgusting to David, they sent and
hired the Syrians of Beth-rehob and of Zobah, 20,000
foot soldiers, and of the king of Maacah 1,000 men,
and of Tob 12,000 men. When David heard of it, he
sent Joab and all the army of the mighty men. And the
Ammonites came out and put the battle in array at
the entrance of the gate, but the Syrians of Zobah and
of Rehob and the men of Tob and Maacah were stationed by themselves in the open country. When Joab
saw that the battlefront was against him before and
behind, he picked some of all the choice men of Israel
and put them in array against the Syrians. The rest
of the men Joab gave over to Abishai his brother, that
he might put them in array against the Ammonites.
Joab said, 'If the Syrians are too strong for me, then
you shall help me; but if the Ammonites are too strong*

*for you, I will come and help you. Be of good courage;
let us play the man for our people and the cities of our
God. And may the Lord do what seems good to Him.'
And Joab and the people who were with him drew near
to battle against the Syrians, and they fled before him.
And when the Ammonites saw that the Syrians had
fled, they also fled before Abishai and entered the city.
So Joab returned from battling against the Ammonites
and came to Jerusalem. When the Syrians saw that
they were defeated by Israel, they gathered together.
Hadadezer sent and brought the Syrians who were beyond the river [Euphrates]; and they came to Helam,
with Shobach, commander of the army of Hadadezer,
leading them. When David was told, he gathered all
Israel, crossed the Jordan, and came to Helam. Then
the Syrians set themselves in array against David
and fought with him. The Syrians fled before Israel,
and David slew of [them] the men of 700 chariots and
40,000 horsemen and smote Shobach captain of their
army, who died there. And when all the kings serving Hadadezer saw that they were defeated by Israel,
they made peace with Israel and served them. So, the
Syrians were afraid to help the Ammonites any more"
(2 Samuel 10:1-19 AMP).*

Duncan went on to say, "There couldn't have been a greater shame or indignity put upon these ambassadors that David sent. This was a mockery of manhood; a direct affront and nose up to the very nature, revelation, and creation of God." Why is this important? It is imperative to understand that to Hebrews the beard was a symbol of manhood and a very sacred one. God affirmed this by forbidding Jews from trimming their bearded corners as the Canaanites did in their customs (Referenced in Leviticus 19:27; 21:5). This tradition was common knowledge; the Canaanites were very familiar with the beliefs and customs of the Hebrews. Hanun's beard-cutting did not just assault these men but was an assault upon God himself through Satan's influence. They were not just treating David's ambassadors with contempt, but they directly insulted David and the God David served, and that is a very dangerous thing to do when dealing with David, the giant slayer.

What reinforces this notion is what this evil king did next. He exposed the nakedness of these men to the world. Why? …to embarrass and humiliate these men? No, it was far more sinister than this. Remember the sign of covenant God gave Abraham that distinguished Hebrew men from the rest of the world? Circumcision was the mark of God's covenant with Abraham and with Israel. Circumcision was then to Hebrews what baptism is today to Christians, the symbol of divine redemption. This was an intense demonic mockery of the image and covenant, and masculinity of God."

The gravity of this sort of development is further understood in the story of Nabal. King David sent men to Nabal to make a request of him. Instead of receiving them honorably he foolishly insulted them with, "Who is David? Many slaves have run away from their masters these days." He also ridiculed them by refusing their request. David's men soon reported this to him. David then commissioned, and personally accompanied, a sword-wielding delegation to visit Nabal with the intention of killing him and every male in his family. The only reason this did not happen is because Abigail, Nabal's wife, intervened with elaborate gifts and a passionate appeal. Nabal lived up to the meaning of his name – "fool."

In many ways, the devil has done the same with men today. He has emasculated them, shamed them, and ridiculed their manhood, making them into fools. In essence, half their beards have been shaved off by media, movies, and society. They have not just cut off their tunics but their gonads as well. Their manhood is laughed at and made the brunt of jokes. But as I said earlier, manhood is not a joke to God. He made man in His own image and that image is great! Therefore, men have greatness in them because He is great. He expects men to be great and to express His mighty masculinity.

Today, men are bombarded on every side by all types of conflicting messages of what real manhood is. This is why so many men feel confused about their masculinity. Because of this, they have no concept of their identity in Christ or purpose in life, and consequently, retreat from the very things God has called them to do and that's to lead, cherish, honor, and defend. The result of Joab and Abishai's stand, according to what we just read, is that it broke the back of the enemy! Distinctive and authentic manhood always breaks the back of the enemy every time it is manifested! As men, we must fight against this onslaught of the enemy and not allow Satan to get away with this. We must line ourselves up as men back to back and say, "No more!" and live out the true masculinity of God on earth.

6

Play the Man

"Be of good courage; let us play the man for our people and the cities of our God"

(2 Samuel 10:12 NKJV).

"We play the man today and the mouse tomorrow."

— C. H. Spurgeon

T his world allows men to be inconsistent. One moment we are strong; the next we are weak. One moment we are happy; the next we are sad. One moment we are courageous; the next we are fearful. We are victims of the "man and mouse syndrome" that Spurgeon alludes to. Walking with God enables us to be consistent in playing the man.

A Man's Work

My dad was the hardest working man I have ever known. As I said earlier, he worked as a longshoreman on the shipping docks of New Orleans. He had the most calloused hands and deepest, widest back you have ever seen. One hot Louisiana summer day while we sat out on our back porch, he looked at our yard and said, "I'm going to build us a pool." As far as anyone knew, he had never built a pool, but that did not stop my dad. However, what he did next shocked everyone. He went into the shed and emerged with a shovel, a pick, string and wooden stakes. He marked out a spot and began shoveling. It took him three months with my older brothers as reluctant helpers to hand dig the pool. No machine, no backhoe, no auger — all back and brawn. As a boy I wanted so much to be like my dad and sweat like him; I would wet my hair and body with the garden hose, so I would look like I was sweating. When the day came for the pouring of the concrete, we had to wheelbarrow it from the street to the backyard one load at a time. He borrowed several wheelbarrows from friends and went to work. I wanted to help so I asked him if I could roll the wheelbarrow. He warned me it was heavy and harder than it looked. I pleaded, "Please, Dad, I can do it." I did pretty well until my spaghetti arms gave out and I flipped over the wheelbarrow full of wet cement. He was not a happy camper, to say the least. He said, "Son, this is a man's work."

At that moment I thought, "I will never be weak again, I will be strong and do a man's work." I believe that's when my drive began for lifting weights. I was ten.

The first time I heard this phrase, "play the man," it was spoken by my same preacher friend, Duncan Brannan. It was the second to the fifteenth-century description of the Hebrew word *Chazaq*, which means to fasten, to seize, to conquer, to be strong, to be courageous, to prove one's valor or to have steeled obedience. For hundreds of years this phrase had been used to rouse men of God to do great exploits amid the most perilous of times.

Andrizo Men

Two stories come to mind where this phrase "play the man" emerges. One was revealed in the Early Christian Writings about St. Polycarp of Smyrna. Polycarp was a beloved bishop and a renowned church father. As the Roman Empire flourished in that part of the world, it became a rough place for Jews and Christians to live. Both Jews and Christians were of monotheistic faith, and the Romans instituted emperor worship, so any-body caught not bowing a knee to an image or idol of Caesar subjected himself to pretty harsh treatment, even death. Born in 70 AD, Polycarp came to believe in Christ at an early age. He had the opportunity later to study directly under the Apostle John the Beloved. John eventually appointed him bishop over the city of Smyrna where he faithfully ministered for many years. The persecution of Christians became more intense under the ruthless Roman emperor, Marcus Aurelius. In the year 156 AD, Roman soldiers arrested Polycarp and took him before the Roman proconsul in Smyrna. He was urged to utter the phrase, "Marcus Aurelius is lord," and offer a small pinch of incense to the statue of the emperor. Such a simple formality would have spared Polycarp from torture and death. His refusal to do so, however, infuriated the bloodthirsty mob. Then, according to Smyrna letters recording the event, as Polycarp was dragged to the place of execution, a voice was heard from heaven by all the believers pres-ent. The voice said, "Be strong, Polycarp, and play the man." Then standing in the arena, Polycarp was urged one last time to renounce Christ. His... statement, well attested in historical accounts was, "Eighty-six years I have served Christ, and He has never done me wrong. How can I blaspheme my King who saved me?" They soon led Polycarp to the stake where they would attempt to burn him alive. Claiming that God would give him the strength to remain on the stake without moving, he asked not to be nailed nor tied to the stake, assuring his persecutors he would not move. He wanted to worship. Then after Polycarp raised his arms in worship and prayer, the fire was kindled. But to the astonishment of the crowd, the flames swirled around him to create an arch over him as if a wall of wind protected him. His body was unscathed by the flame, and a sweet-smelling aroma filled the air. The executor was then ordered to plunge a spear through the flames into Polycarp. After doing so, as the letter records, Polycarp's blood gushed forth extinguishing the flames. One of early Christianity's most important church fathers was dead. His life and death exemplified a genuine testimony of faith that would endure for thousands of years.

But the death of Polycarp backfired, for his conviction and witness went on to inspire and embolden thousands of saints after him. He is a tangible illustration of what it means to be an authentic man in the face of the enemy and break Satan's power over true manhood.

The other story is found in the *Foxe's Book of Martyrs*. In the fifteenth century, there were two beloved bishops of the time named Nicolas Ridley and Hugh Latimer. The place was Oxford, England. Like Polycarp, they, too, found themselves commanded to compromise their beliefs or die, but this time under the cruel hands of Queen Mary. When they wouldn't denounce their beliefs, they were bound to a stake to be burned alive. With their hands tied together and their backs to each other Latimer said to Ridley, "Be of good cheer, Ridley; and play the man. We shall this day, by God's grace, light up such a candle in England, as I trust, shall never be put out."

A few years ago, my pastor, Mike Hayes, visited Oxford and noticed an unpaved patch on one of the main roads in the center of town. When he asked why, the local guide said, "Oh, that's where Latimer and Ridley were burned at the stake for their faith," and then led him to a plaque on the wall of a building that told the story. He took a picture of himself standing on the very spot and sent it to me, knowing my fondness of the story. As I looked at the picture my chest swelled up with manly pride as I thought, the candle of authentic manhood is still lit.

Today we don't use the phrase "play the man," we use phrases like "man up" or "you're the man." It's the same thing. Why are the words "play the man" so foreign to us? It is because playing the man has become a lost art! The world no longer knows what it is to play the man because demonstrations of distinctive and authentic manhood have become so scarce! It's like hunting for rare game: It's precious when sighted, but seldom caught—much less seen up close. Our country is in such need of real men, and God is moving in our midst again. He searches for men to play the man!

In Second Chronicles it says, "For the eyes of the LORD run to and fro throughout the whole earth, to show Himself strong on behalf of those whose heart is loyal to Him" (2 Chronicles 16:9 NKJV). This scripture again uses the word *Chazaq* for the word "strong," which, as you know, is Andrizo in Greek. God is looking for men today through whom He can play the man! He's looking for Andrizo men!

Will you be that man?

The Magnificent Five

"Man skills may get you man points, but manhood virtues get you God points"

—Mark Batterson

"Only seven yet they fought like seven hundred."

—The Magnificent Seven poster

O ur society does a great job reinforcing human performance. We applaud people who make a lot of money. We praise people who look good, people who speak well, and people who live well. Men have many ways of earning "man points." On the other hand, those points diminish with every passing moment because they are not rooted in the virtues of God. One of my favorite old western movies is called *The Magnificent Seven*. It stars Yul Brynner, Steve McQueen, and Charles Bronson, to mention a few. It is about a peaceful Mexican village at the mercy of Calvera, the leader of a band of outlaws. The townspeople, too afraid to fight for themselves, hire seven American gunslingers to save them from the yearly raid of bandits. The gunslingers train the villagers to defend themselves and then plan a trap for the evil Calvera and his gang. They eventually defeat them, but in the process many of the gunslingers perish. It embodies an extraordinary example of bravery, honor, and sacrifice. That's why I loved the movie and why I decided, when I ran across five extraordinary virtues or pillars for manhood in the book of First Corinthians, I titled it "The Magnificent Five."

I teach these five virtues or pillars at our men's retreats. Today thousands of men have heard and learned these virtues, and it has transformed their lives. As I said in the earlier chapters, the Apostle Paul finds himself in a challenging spot. He's two-hundred miles away and has left in Corinth those he felt were the best men to oversee this young, growing church. The reports, however, are troubling. One such report includes a young man sleeping around with his stepmother and coming to church as if nothing was wrong (see 1 Corinthians 5:1-7). The leaders of the church stuck their heads in the sand as if it would all go away. But as the old saying goes, "All sin needs to thrive is for good men to do nothing." Well, Paul wasn't going to stand for it, so he writes these letters to bring some clarity to the nonsense of their denial and passivity. In 1 Corinthians 16:13-14 he lays out five virtues of manhood for them including the admonishment to, "Act like men." The only problem is they have no idea what that looks like, and here in lies the problem even today. Men are confused about how real men should act.

As quoted earlier, we live in an androgynous society. This means that people are confused about which gender to be or which sex roles to play. Men seem to be often confused about what manhood is. According to modern-day sociology and social psychology, there is an acceptable trend in America that allows a "new freedom" for men and women to be and act as the opposite gender or both genders. As a result, men often don't know whether to be nice guys or tough guys. They don't know whether to be aggressive or passive. Part of this confusion may stem from the absence of a father and having been raised exclusively by mothers who wouldn't let them play with guns or swords, even in make-believe. "It is too violent," I heard one mother say as she scolded her son for using a metal trash lid for a shield and sawed-off broomstick for a sword. What she didn't seem to realize was that part of our make up in God is the "warrior spirit." Man is made from an image of a warrior who is a perfect blend of power, honor, courage, and compassion. Numerous scriptural passages spell out that man is unique and has a unique role to play as a man. These include Exodus 15:3, Isaiah 42:13, Romans 8:37, and 2 Timothy 2:3-5, and many more.

Toxic Masculinity

I once read an article written by Focus on the Family about feminist Karla Mantilla who tried summarizing the philosophy of "Toxic Masculinity" and its mindset in an article she wrote entitled "Kids Need 'Fathers' Like Fish Need Bicycles." She wrote, "I submit that men tend to emphasize values such as discipline, power, control, stoicism and independence. Sure, there can be some good from these things, but they are mostly damaging to kids (and other living things). They certainly made my son suffer an isolated and tortured existence until he began to see that there was a way out of the trap of masculinity."

The trap of masculinity? Are you kidding me? It

is masculinity that we need again in this country. But this is the way many feminists view maleness. A centerpiece of this hostility is seen in an ongoing effort to convince us that "men are fools." It claims that the majority of males are immature, impulsive, selfish, weak and not very bright. It is interesting to note, for example, how disrespect for men pervades the entertainment industry. I recently watched another DC or Marvel movie with my kids and that's the profile they always follow. I hate it! I could fill a book with other examples of man-bashing in today's culture. Chief among them is the curricula of university women's studies programs whose central theme is hatred and ridicule of men. Roger Scruton, author of "Modern Manhood," explained what is happening to perceptions of masculinity. "Feminists have sniffed out male pride wherever it has grown and ruthlessly uprooted it. Under their pressure, modern culture has downgraded or rejected such masculine virtues as courage, tenacity and military prowess in favor of more gentler, more 'socially inclusive' habits."

Recently a friend of mine, Tripp Davis, sent me an article he ran across about a dangerous movement called non-binary. Binary means relating or involving two things. In this case, it refers to male and female. So, to be non-binary is to reject the fact that you are male or female. Non-binaries reject gender pronouns like he or she and want to be referred to as they or they're.

Several countries are already adopting these broader gender definitions. Nepal, India, Pakistan, Bangladesh, Germany, New Zealand, and Australia all allow citizens to legally identify themselves as a third gender. It's rumored that Thailand's new constitution will also include a third gender. Recently, more than 100,000 people signed a petition that asked the White House to expand its definition of gender. The petitioners wanted to include transgender, agender, genderfluid, pangender, among others. Brown University now offers classes on "Toxic Masculinity." With this in mind; the question is not if the U.S. government will follow suit, but when.

Again, this is all strategic by Satan to drive home his plan of de-masculinization of men. Satan hates the image of God and wants with all his might to tarnish and ultimately destroy that image. It is vital that we as men made in His image be authentic and distinctive men. That is the premise of this book. Men, we desperately need to stand up and fight this spirit and show the world how real men act. It's not this egotistical, chauvinistic, macho man. It's T.N.T "Tough and Tender" as my friend, Pastor Ricky Texada says.

Corporate psychologist Dr. Tim Irwin, vice president of Right Management Consulting, has observed these same trends in business settings. They have resulted in what he calls "the feminization of the workplace." Irwin said the effort to end sexual harassment and discrimination, which has been a legitimate concern that needed to be addressed, has placed great political power in the hands of women. A man's career can be ruined by even the implication, valid or invalid, that he has treated a female employee disrespectfully.

The bottom line is that many men have lost their compass. Not only do they not know who they are, they're not sure what the culture expects them to be . . . It is time that men acted like men – being respectful, thoughtful and gentlemanly to women, but reacting with confidence, strength and certainty in manner. Some have *wimped out*, acting like whipped puppies. Others have boldly *spoken out* against feminist influence, refusing to be intimidated by the advocates of political correctness. Some have *lashed out*, reacting with anger and frustration. Some have *flamed out*, resorting to alcohol, drugs, illicit sex and other avenues of escape. Some have *copped out,* descending into mindless TV, professional sports and obsessive recreational activities. Some have *sold out,* becoming advocates of the new identity. Some have simply *walked out,* leaving their families in a lurch. Many, however, seem placidly unaware that they have lost their place in the culture. The result is a changing view of manhood with far-reaching implications for the future of the family."

Despite the fact that men were designed by their Creator to fulfill these critical and unique roles, our culture remains resolute in its determination to strip away the very essence of what it means to be a man. If you're a father, I urge you to do everything within your power to model healthy masculinity for your son. And if you're a single mom, please make every effort to find healthy male role models for your boys, perhaps at church or through your extended family. If you leave it to the schools and the media to teach your son what it means to be a man, you will be subjecting your precious little one to potentially irreparable harm.

The spirit of a warrior should not be stifled in a boy. Otherwise, when he becomes a man, he may be weak, powerless, confused and unable to handle adversity or responsibility.

Where are our strong men, whose character outweighs their talent? We have so many talented and gifted men who cannot hold on to a job or a marriage because they have been so pampered and sheltered that the minute they encounter stress or pain they cave in. We need good models of well-rounded men. We need to see how they act.

So, Paul in his letter to the Corinthian church goes there and begins to give us a model of how a man should act. He gives us five of the most powerful virtues of distinctive and authentic manhood I have ever read. In his book, *Play the Man,* Pastor Mark Batterson shares the seven virtues he feels best describe manhood. Tough love, childlike wonder, will power, raw passion, true grit, clear vision and moral courage. I love them all and completely agree with them, but the five I found in this Corinthian passage are the ones I live by and choose to focus on: vigilance, conviction, courage, strength, and compassion. In the next few chapters I will break each one down in detail so you can apply them to your life and experience the powerful transformation that thousands of others have experienced.

8

Men of Vigilance

"Be alert and on your guard; stand firm in your faith; act like men and be courageous; grow in strength! Let everything you do be done in love…"

(1 Corinthians 16:13-14 NLT).

"Freedom is the virtue of the vigilant."

—James deMelo

"We must be vigilant, even of each other, but mostly of ourselves."

—Viet Thanh Nguyen

"Be sober, be vigilant; because your adversary the devil walks about like a roaring lion, seeking whom he may devour."

—St. Peter

Destiny My Heart Cried

To continue the story I alluded to in the preface, I write that it was a beautiful day in Lake City,

Michigan. My friend, Rusty, and I had spent the night with a friend at his cabin by the lake. We planned to do some fishing that day, but the lake was too rough, so we decided to do some scouting for the upcoming hunting season. The forest was exceptionally beautiful on this April day; it seemed to be in full glory, with the flowers blooming, trees budding and animals chattering. Even Rusty, who is not a hunter, seemed to enjoy it. Afterward, we ate an early dinner together before heading back to Grand Rapids. Little did we know what evil lurked, looking for whom he could devour!

"Look out!" my friend screamed, but it was too late. I never saw the semi-truck until it hit us. It happened so fast, all I could do was close my eyes and pray. "Destiny," I cried, "I still have a destiny to fulfill, Father. You are faithful to complete what You began in me!"

Silence.

I heard a faint groaning sound from my badly injured friend. I wanted to help him, but my body would not move. I could smell the mixture of radiator fluid and oil. I could not see because of the glass in my eyes.

My mind flashed back to the summer of 1970. I was seven years old and swimming in a lake with my cousin and barely knew how to swim. After splashing in the shallow end of the lake for a few hours, my uncle offered to swim us on his back to where my two older sisters were jumping off a floating dock about fifty yards out. My uncle left us with my sisters to supervise. They weren't too happy because they were busy trying to catch some cute boy's attention. The lake was deep on this end, so I didn't venture off too far from the dock, but when my sister made a comment about how poor my swimming was, I decided I would show her. When she turned her back, I jumped in with a plan to swim to shore. I didn't make it. About halfway there I ran out of steam and started to panic. Fear gripped me so tight I couldn't even scream for help, and with hundreds of people in this little marked out swimming area, the one lifeguard had his hands full. I remember just a few feet from me someone floated in an innertube, but I could not reach it, or scream for help, because of fear. I was sinking, cold water rushed into my lungs, and then I felt the bottom of the lake underneath my feet. I looked up and saw the light shining from the surface, it was beautiful but frightening at the same time. Slowly I start to suffocate and blackout.

All of a sudden, I felt someone grab me by the hair

and pull me up to the shore. My sister had swum to where my cousin had pointed–where he last saw me. After frantically searching for me on the surface, she searched the bottom, touched my hair and pulled me to safety. The odds of her finding me in that crowded lake with zero visibility was a miracle, but God was not finished with me yet; I had a destiny.

Next came a memory of me at age seventeen and under my car working to remove a drive shaft. The jack slipped and began to slowly sink into the soft Louisiana soil. I was pinned before I could get out. The frame of the car was crushing my chest, with every attempted breath, I was suffocating. Fear gripped me again; I began to scream for help. My father who had gotten home early that day from work, (a rare occurrence), heard me from inside the house and came running to lift the car and pull me out. Again, God was not finished with me yet; I had a destiny.

Returning to the present I was injured and stuck in a mangled vehicle. I was suffocating again. With every breath I felt my life slipping away, my heartbeat was slowing down, three heartbeats then two and then nothing. Silence again, but this time it was different. Pitch darkness surrounded me, but fear was not present. I was not afraid. I sensed something in the darkness with me — death close by; but I was still unafraid. Fear was completely absent. Someone else occupied the moment there with me; I couldn't see Him, but I could feel Him. Peace flooded my soul, a freedom I had never experienced before. I knew I had stepped into another realm. I thought, "I must be dead, and soon I will see Jesus and my mother," I began to scream out their names. Over and over I screamed, "Jesus, let me see you! Mom! Mom!" But I was held back, waiting for something. For what? I didn't know.

Suddenly I heard a voice say, "You called me faithful, and faithful I AM." At that moment I felt pulled back like a roller coaster in reverse. "What is your name?" the strange voice asked. Back in my body, I could hear people all around me. "Sir, what is your name?" the voice asked again. "Reverend James deMelo," I answered. Why I used "reverend" before my name, I don't know. I had never referred to myself as reverend before. Maybe I was unconsciously making a statement to the death spirit which encircled me that, "I am a man of God, and you're not taking me unless He says so."

The next hours were a blur, but one thing I remember

very clearly: the voice of my wife. Somehow, she got through to me at the local hospital before they flew me to Grand Rapids. "Misty, it's bad," I told her.

"James, listen to me. You have destiny to fulfill. You hear me? You have a destiny!" Destiny. There's that word again. There was strength in her voice and, somehow, I knew I was going to be okay.

I would later come to find out the extent of my injuries and all that had transpired—it is an undeniable miracle that I am alive! My neck was broken in the same place as actor Christopher Reeve, but my spinal cord was only bruised. Several bones in my back, ribs, my left wrist and left shoulder blade, were all broken. My friend, Rusty, was in an induced coma due to his head injuries. Fourteen days later he came out of his coma and slowly recovered. Thirteen days later I walked out of the hospital and spent three months in a halo brace rehabbing. Destiny had prevailed! After returning home, I learned more about the events surrounding the accident. Mike Rustle, a highly trained paramedic in town, stood at the exact corner of the collision. In fact, he saw the whole thing happen. When he reached the truck, I was without a heartbeat and had no signs of life. From the look of my limp neck and the blood coming from my mouth, nose, and ears, he knew he needed to make some quick critical measures to revive me. When I met him later to thank him he pulled me aside. He told me that as he pulled me out of the truck, he heard the words, "This man must not die!" It startled him. He felt God's hand guiding him. All this reassures me that God is in constant watch over His children. He says in His word, "He will not leave you nor forsake you" (Deuteronomy 31:6 NKJV). Later I was asked to speak at his church and share my testimony, where he recommitted his life to Christ.

I share this story because it could have, perhaps, been avoided if I had just exercised more vigilance. You see, I pulled out in front of that truck. I didn't see it. God was trying to warn me that morning and prompted me to pray, but I got distracted by the company. I blew through "spiritual red lights" way before the physical ones. That's why I find it interesting that the first thing Paul says is, "Be alert and on your guard." Paul goes to the very principle that man violated in the beginning. If you remember, Adam had the responsibility as the watchman of the Garden of Eden and that included his wife, Eve. When Satan tempted Eve where was Adam?

"Now the serpent was more cunning than any beast of the field which the LORD God had made. And he said to the woman, 'Has God indeed said, "You shall not eat of every tree of the garden?"' And the woman said to the serpent, 'We may eat the fruit of the trees of the garden; but of the fruit of the tree which is in the midst of the garden, God has said, "You shall not eat it, nor shall you touch it, lest you die."' Then the serpent said to the woman, 'You will not surely die. For God knows that in the day you eat of it your eyes will be opened, and you will be like God, knowing good and evil.' So when the woman saw that the tree was good for food, that it was pleasant to the eyes, and a tree desirable to make one wise, she took of its fruit and ate. She also gave to her husband with her, and he ate" (Genesis 3:1-6 NKJV).

Notice she didn't have to go looking for him; he was right there with her. You mean that knucklehead stood right there and listened to the serpent deceive his wife? Yes! And did nothing about it! Talk about a bonehead. But wait; before we condemn Adam, how many times have we done this? How many times have we been so absorbed with work, sports, and "busyness" that we come home and are totally oblivious to our wife's struggles or the children's needs? How many times do we avoid deep conversations with them because we are too tired and don't want to deal with it? Or we don't want to hear the truth? Passivity and lack of responsibility in this area are among the greatest sins of man. Adam, not Eve, was given the truth and instructions about the tree of life. He had the responsibility of caring for the Garden of Eden and protecting his wife. But when the enemy came in and deceived his wife, he just stood there and did nothing. This is called the sin of omission, and many men fall into its trap all the time.

We are called to be "watchmen." The Greek word Paul uses for vigilance or watchman is the word *gregoreo*, which means to be awake, to be watchful, or to be vigilant. It refers to a watchful spiritual attitude and can be translated, "Be wide-eyed awake," rather than go to sleep on the job. It's taken from the root word *egiro* which means, "One who collects his faculties and is aroused from obscurity or inactivity." It is one who arises or rears up and takes a stand.

The job of the watchman in the Old Testament was

to sit on the city wall and constantly scan the horizon for enemies. Therefore, they had to stay alert. They were the first line of defense from an attacking army; they were the eyes and ears for the protection of the city. Therefore, Paul exhorts us, "Stay awake! Stay on your guard, keep your eyes open!" Both Paul and Peter talked about men who are willing to stand up with their back to the wall and say, "No one will hurt you on my watch because I will stay vigilant!"

Like the Corinthians, men today are asleep at the wheel of their destiny, and the Spirit of God is encouraging us through Paul to awaken to a holy alertness. We must continually be aware of our surroundings because it is paramount to our manhood and survival in this spiritual battle. In Second Corinthians, Paul goes on to say that we are not to be ignorant of Satan's devices (2 Corinthians 2:11). It baffles me how men can be so oblivious or unaware of Satan's schemes and sly ways when the Bible is full of warnings.

Did you know that one of God's criteria for choosing Gideon's 300 mighty warriors comes from this very principle? When we find Gideon in Judges chapter six, he is alone, fearful, and has a very low self-esteem. But God calls the mighty man of valor out of this timid man and gives him an army of 300 bad-to-the-bone warriors. But he didn't start off with 300; he started with 32,000. The faint-hearted were cut first, they were told to go home and 22,000 left. The second cut was a little more interesting.

> *"But the LORD said to Gideon, 'There are still too many men. Take them down to the water, and I will sift them for you there. If I say, "This one shall go with you," he shall go; but if I say, "This one shall not go with you," he shall not go.' So Gideon took the men down to the water. There the LORD told him, 'Separate those who lap the water with their tongues like a dog from those who kneel down to drink.' Three hundred men lapped with their hands to their mouths. All the rest got down on their knees to drink. The LORD said to Gideon, 'With the three hundred men that lapped I will save you and give the Midianites into your hands. Let all the other men go, each to his own place.' So Gideon sent the rest of the Israelites to their tents but kept the three hundred, who took over the provisions and trumpets of the others. Now the camp of Midian lay below him in the valley" (Judges 7:4-8 ESV).*

What was this about? Well, if you're a "military guy," you know exactly what this was about. Any military guy knows water holes are prime locations for potential ambushes of the enemy, especially during battle time and in desert conditions. So, no smart warrior approaches a waterhole during battle carelessly. They keep their eyes on the horizon and approach cautiously. God weeds them out by observing how they drink water from the river. The ones who thrust their heads in the river and drink with no regard for their surroundings or their fellow brothers in battle are sent home. But the ones who cup the water and bring it up to their mouths to lap it, keeping their eyes on the horizon, and displaying an awareness of the potential of the enemy's propensity to ambush at water holes — these are the ones God chose.

Trophy Hunting

I'm an avid bow hunter, and several years back I enjoyed a hunting opportunity of a lifetime. After we conducted an evangelistic mission trip in South Africa, several pastor friends and myself were given a hunting trip. It was an amazing experience, but one of the things I learned about bow hunting in Africa is that most of it is done in small blinds over water holes. One morning a whole heard of impalas came in. As my heart began to race, and I started to focus in on an animal, the guide told me to wait. I asked him why. That's when he told me, "The big mature trophy ones don't come in right away; they're smart, very leery and cautious, that's why they're old. These you see now are all younger, inexperienced and stupid. Wait and you will see the bigger ones come in later. They stay hidden in shadows of the trees." In my office today, I have a gold medal record impala because of that lesson. That experience helped me understand the story of Gideon and the importance of vigilance.

God knew who Gideon needed. Not the fearful, immature and unobservant ones, but the ones who would keep their eyes locked on the horizon watching for the enemy. They were the alert ones who understood the enemy's tactics. They were the type of men with whom you would want to go into battle — not the self-preservationist, but a man who would have your back. They were the ones who in God's eyes were worthy of fighting alongside Gideon.

The Praying Man

"Being vigilant is being prayerful, which leads to being thankful in the long run." —Pastor Mike Hayes

As I said earlier, the morning of the accident I felt a strong pull to pray and dismissed it because of the company and a very busy schedule. How I wish I had been vigilant and prayed that morning. Who knows what could have changed? It might have saved so much pain and suffering. That's why, when my middle daughter a few years ago went through a tough time, I was there alert and praying. My daughter Makayla is a great athlete and played soccer most of her young life. When the call of God came, she had a decision to follow her dream or God's dream. She chose God's dream, but then the enemy came quickly, bringing confusion, depression, and doubt. She vacillated for months, locking herself in her room for days at a time. I became very concerned for her and began to pray.

One night, awakened by the Holy Spirit, I walked out of my room and saw her light on. I felt that same pull to pray, and so I did. The next night it happened again, and while I was praying in my home office, I heard her walking around in her room, which was above my office. I felt the leading of the Holy Spirit to go up and knock on her door and had a chance to sit with her for hours talking, crying and feeling her hurt and pain. I was able to share with her my own struggles when

God called me out of bodybuilding and into ministry and that I related to what she was experiencing. Today my daughter is full of life and vision and attends Oral Roberts University. After we talked and prayed that night, she had an opportunity to share her testimony with the youth. So, you could imagine my shock when she mentioned having suicidal thoughts and, between a conversation with her father and the Holy Spirit, she successfully fought it off to gain peace over her heart and mind. Her mother and I sat in tears and were so thankful to the Holy Spirit who led me to pray that morning for her, and that I was vigilant enough to hear Him and protect my daughter's heart.

Prayer sees things before they happen and diffuses the enemy's plans. Men who pray see things before others see them. As far as I see it, there are two ways to live your life: survival mode or prayerful mode! Dr. Edwin Louis Cole used to say, "As men we are to direct, correct and protect, to guide, guard and govern, to be the prophet, priest, and king of our homes." King of our homes doesn't mean we are to lord it over our spouses but, ultimately, we are responsible for all that goes on in our homes, under our care and domain. Therefore, we are the first line of defense and prayer is the catalyst.

The Family Man

Psalm 128 gives the perfect formula for vigilance over your family and the happiness it brings to your home. "When you eat the labor of your hands, you shall be happy, and it shall be well with you. Your wife shall be like a fruitful vine in the very heart of your house, your children like olive plants all around your table. Behold, thus shall the man be blessed (happy) who fears the LORD. The LORD bless you out of Zion, And may you see the good of Jerusalem all the days of your life" (Psalm 128:2-5 NKJV).

Let me unpack this for you: "Your wife shall be like a fruitful vine." Here we see the importance of being vigilant over our spouse. Husbandry in horticultural terms means the work of a gardener. According to this scripture, our wives should be like fruitful vines. If you ever planted flowery vines, then you know they need trellises. You can't just throw it in the ground and expect it to blossom and grow. It might survive and curl around a few rocks and sticks, but if you build a trellis and place its vines on the lattice, you will see a beautiful display of colors and growth. A good gardener also cultivates the soil in which he plants the seed. He waters it, fertilizes it, and as it grows, prunes it, weeds it, and keeps the bugs off.

I can't tell you how many times I have had men in my office wringing their hands and weeping, saying, 'I don't know what happened. She's gone, she filed for divorce.' This is why they say eighty percent of all divorces filed in the U.S. are filed by women, with the man left clueless. That tells you a lot regarding where men are in this area of vigilance.

If it's not the wife, it's the kids; if it's not the kids, it's work, health or fill in the blank. It's the negligence of not building a godly trellis. When your wife and children have nothing to build on, nothing to grab ahold of in the way of godly principles, then the consequences are devastating. Men, my point is we need to wake up and smell the coffin the enemy tries to build for our family. We need to understand the enemy is a master of deception, a chameleon of chameleons. He knows how to change fifty shades of color. He has been doing it for thousands of years. What makes us think we can squirrel through life and not pay the price? Men, I submit that one of our greatest responsibilities as men according to God is to create such an atmosphere in our homes that our wives blossom and our children spring up as olive plants. "Your children are like olive plants all around your table." Here we are to be vigilant over our children. Olive trees in Israel are the producers of the anointing oil and one of great commerce. Therefore, these olive trees are well cared for and protected. It's a hardy tree and has withstood thousands of years of fire, wind, and drought. Our children are likened to this tree and, like the oil it produces, our children are an extension of our anointing. Next time you sit down to eat dinner with your children, think of this and how you are helping them grow stronger in character and faith. For they need to know God doesn't test our strength on the outside, but our strength on the inside.

"The Lord bless you out of Zion." This is speaking of vigilance over our jobs. Zion is where David lived. This worshiper, and also this warrior, went out and conquered and brought back the spoils to his house and to the house of the Lord. Notice, in the beginning, it says, "When you eat the labor of your hands, you shall be happy, and it shall be well with you." This is talking about work and the implications it has on our lives and in the Kingdom.

"And may you see the good of Jerusalem." Here we see the importance of exercising vigilance over

God's house. Jerusalem is always depicted as a type of church in scripture. Jerusalem is where the first temple was built. We are to see to it that goodness comes forth from our church. There is so much "bad-mouthing" of the church today. I know the church has not been perfect, because people are not perfect, but we must understand that the only hope for the world is the church. Everything good in my life has come from the church. I was saved in a church. I met my wife in a church; my kids were saved and dedicated in a church. Has the church hurt me? Yes, but I have been hurt by my wife as well, but I don't leave her. The only way to experience the goodness of the church is to take care of her, to speak well of her and to serve her. Then you can receive the goodness of the church and share that goodness. Tithing is one of the ways to see the goodness of the church spread to the world. As I said, the only hope of the world is the church, but I add, the only hope of the church is true disciples.

The Heart of Man

I cannot stress enough the importance of vigilance over your heart. The Bible says, "Keep vigilant watch over your heart; that's where life starts" (Proverbs 4:20

MSG). Everything emanates, begins with and is initiated by the heart. Scripture always prioritized the heart because unless your heart is completely and totally devoted to what you're doing, you're wasting your time. Unless the heart comes first, there will be no real catalytic change in the life of an individual. This is why we can't flippantly give our heart to just anyone or anything without serious thought to how that would affect our future.

Did you know in some medical circles the heart is considered the second brain? Dr. Pearsall in his book, *The Heart's Code,* shared a haunting story of a little girl who had received a heart transplant. Shortly afterward, she began to have extreme nightmares of strangulation and violence. When the nightmares continued, and the imagery became very vivid, they brought in some experts who then called the police who, through the details given by the little girl, were able to apprehend a murderer who, as yet, had not been brought to justice. The girl's parents came to discover the transplanted heart came from a little girl who had been raped, beaten and strangled to death.

Our heart is a reservoir of greatness or sadness and holds the key to life; that's why we need to care for and protect it at all cost. A friend and mentor, Rick Renner, once said that we are the bishop of our hearts and then quoted Hebrews 12:15. It says, "Looking diligently, lest any man fails of the grace of God; lest any root of bitterness springing up trouble you, and thereby many are defiled." The words "looking diligently" in this verse is the Greek word *episkopos*. It means *"to look over"* or *"to take supervisory oversight."* The word *episkopos* is the same Greek word translated "bishop" in First Timothy 3:1. As you know, a bishop has *oversight* or *responsibility* for a group of churches. As the chief overseer for those churches, it is the bishop's responsibility to *watch, direct, guide, correct,* and *give oversight* to the churches under his care. As long as he serves as bishop, he is held responsible for the *good* and the *bad* that occurs under his ministry. Hebrews 12:15 uses the word *episkopos* to alert you and me to the fact that *we are the bishops of our own hearts.* The use of this word in the verse means it is our responsibility to *watch, direct, guide, correct,* and *give oversight* to what goes on inside us. As the bishop of your own heart, it is your responsibility to give oversight to what goes on inside your emotions and thinking. You alone are responsible for what you allow to develop inside your head and heart.

As a bishop, you are personally responsible for both the good and the bad that occurs within your thought life.

Why do I make this point? This is important because we are often tempted to blame our *bad attitudes, bitterness, resentments, or feelings of unforgiveness* on other people. But the truth is we are responsible for our own emotions and reactions! If a person does something that has the potential to offend us, God holds *us* responsible for whether or not that offense takes root in our hearts. We can choose to let it sink into our souls and take root, or we can opt to let it bypass us. We are not able to control what others do or say to us, but we *can* control what goes on *inside* us.

It is that "inside" part—*the part you control*—for which God will hold you responsible. Why? You are charged with a personal responsibility to *oversee* what goes on inside your heart. That means *you* have the last word. You are the one who decides whether or not that wrong settles down into your heart and starts to take root in your emotions. Anger is an emotion that comes and goes. You *choose* whether or not irritation turns into *anger*, anger into *wrath*, wrath into *bitterness*, bitterness into *resentment*, and resentment into *unforgiveness*. You *choose* whether these foul attitudes and emotions take up residency in your heart or are booted out the door!

When the devil comes to tempt you with annoying, hounding thoughts about the person who offended you, at that moment the choice of whether or not it sinks in is totally up to you. You are the *only* one who can give permission for these attitudes to make their habitation in your mind and emotions. If you are filled with *bitterness, resentment,* and *unforgiveness,* you *permit* the devil to sow that destructive seed in your heart, and then you *permit* it to grow. Remember, you're the bishop of your own heart!

There is only one reason weeds grow out of control in a garden—because no one took the proper time and care to uproot and remove them. When the garden is choked by weeds, the gardener can't complain, "I don't know how this happened! How did this occur right under my nose?" It was his irresponsibility that caused it to occur. If the proper amount of vigilance had been exercised, he would have known weeds were about to get the best of him. His *lack of vigilance* is the reason his garden got into this mess!

Hebrews 12:15 says, "Looking *diligently...*" It takes *diligence* to keep your heart in good shape. The only way you can stay free of the weeds the devil wants to sow in your "garden" is to be attentive, careful, thorough, and meticulous about the condition of your own heart. Don't expect others to take care of your heart. It's *your* heart, and you are the only one with authority to decide what does and does not go on inside you. In light of this truth, what are you going to do about the situation you face right now? Forgive and let it go, or hang on to that grievance and let it grow? *The choice is yours!*

The Mind of Man

"The mind is a terrible thing to waste" as the old commercial goes, but I'm telling you, not only is it a waste, but it is the primary battle zone of the enemy, and we are to protect it at all cost. This is why Second Corinthians says, "We use our powerful God-tools for smashing warped philosophies, tearing down barriers erected against the truth of God, fitting every loose thought and emotion and impulse into the structure of life shaped by Christ" (2 Corinthians 10:5 MSG). Paul goes on to say, "Don't let the world squeeze you into its own mold, but let God remold your mind from within" (Romans 12:2 ESV).

Caroline Leaf is a cognitive neuroscientist with a Ph.D. in Communication Pathology specializing in Neuropsychology. She also is a strong follower of Christ. In her book, *Who Switched Off My Brain,* she says that up to ninety-five percent of physical and mental health issues are a direct result of your thought life. She talks about the importance of understanding how the brain works and that when we allow negative thoughts to form in our minds, they build what neuroscientists call dendrites (neurons). They are tree-like branches that form in our minds from toxic or non-toxic thoughts. She says the two most fundamental survival mechanisms in our bodies are protection and growth. Our brain and nervous system control both. She likens our brain to a CEO of an organization. A CEO has to grow a company and protect it from internal and external threats, or the company (in our case, our body) will have major problems. She created a system called "Brain Sweep" that helps you remap your brain; she identifies twelve of the most toxic dendrite branches which she calls the "Dirty Dozen." She says that if properly executed, in twenty-one days you can rewire your thought patterns and create a new channel of healthy thinking, acting, and living. All this science proves what the Holy Spirit already gave us in scripture where He warns us to protect our minds and gives us the formula to take down the toxic thoughts by rejecting them as soon as they come and then replacing them with non-toxic thoughts.

"Summing it all up, friends, I'd say you'll do best to fill your minds and meditate on things true, noble, reputable, authentic, compelling, gracious — the best, not the worst; the beautiful, not the ugly; things to praise, not things to curse" (Philippians 4:8 MSG).

Pastor Amie Hayes Dockery once said, "Don't let your internal demotion sabotage your external promotion." My wife used to say to our children when they were young, "Say what you want, not what you feel." All this is good advice on how to exercise vigilance over the mind.

The Purpose of Man

"When Jacob awoke from his sleep, he thought, "Surely the Lord was in this place, and I was not aware of it" (Genesis 28:16 NKJV).

Moses' destiny was activated by this very principle. Moses, if you remember, lived in Midian and went out one day with his flock. He climbed a familiar mountain in the area, Mount Sinai. I've heard people say that the burning bush Moses saw was God's way to get Moses' attention. But I wonder if the burning bush was not an attention-getter, but rather God's way of testing Moses, to see if he became aware of what was all around him. The question is not whether the bush got Moses' attention, but rather, how long it took Moses to notice that the bush was not burning up. I have heard in Israel there is a desert shrub that exudes a certain vapor that can cause it to spontaneously burst into flames if it's hot enough. My point is, it may not have been an impossible thing for Moses to see a burning bush. What made this bush different was that it did not burn up. Moses would have had to stop and take in the sight and watch for a while. The bush was on fire. The bush was still burning. But the fire was not consuming the bush. Only when God noticed that Moses was in tune with what was going on around him did He speak to him. That's fascinating to me, to think God was waiting for Moses to become fully aware so He could awaken him to his destiny. What destiny could we miss by not exercising vigilance of our surroundings in God?

The Old Testament speaks of a tribe of men who

were called Issachar who joined King David's army. "And of the children of Issachar, which were men that had an understanding of the times, to know what Israel ought to do; the heads of them were two hundred, and all their brethren were at their commandment" (1 Chronicles 12:32 KJV). The meaning of their name, Issachar, is "God will surely bring a reward." They were men of great understanding. Men who could separate themselves mentally from the distractions of the world. Men who could rightly distinguish truth—who were cunning, diligent, and prudent. The word "know" in this scripture means *to ascertain by seeing*. The Hebrew word here is *yada*. It is a God-given personal touch of understanding and revelation, birthed out of intimacy with God. In other words, it's not a knowing that comes from reading a book, but firsthand knowledge by drawing near to God. These men helped David discern the times and what God was saying and doing. What an anointing! An anointing I pray I can have and to give to the men I mentor, for this is the purpose of men, to seek God out and to help others to do the same.

9

Men of Convictions

"Keep your eyes open, hold tight to your convictions, give it all you've got, be resolute..."

(1 Corinthians 16:13 MSG).

"A belief is something you will argue about. A conviction is something you will die for!"

—Howard Hendricks

A great scene in the movie, *Braveheart,* consists of William Wallace at the Sterling Battle inspiring men with a speech to charge into battle against great odds. He and his men are painted with blue war paint and have a lion-like face resolved to destroy the enemy. The reason he gives the speech is because the men were losing heart and were beginning to leave. The nobles tried to encourage them to wait until they had negotiated with the English. Their spineless, "conviction-lacking" speech did not affect the men. Only when William showed up with his mighty warriors did he change the outcome of the battle.

Men of conviction will always do that. Paul was one of those men, and that's why he exhorts us to, "Stand firm in the faith" (1 Corinthians 16:13 NLT). As men, we are to have unmovable, unshakable, steadfast faith. The Bible says that it's impossible to please God without faith (Hebrews 11:6). We can't afford to have faulty faith! Someone once said, "If your faith fizzles before the finish, it was faulty from the first." The Bible says, "A righteous man who falters before the wicked is like a murky spring and a polluted well" (Proverbs 25:26 NKJV). Notice he says, a righteous man, basically a church-going man. It says he becomes contaminated when he is indecisive in the face of temptation. When a man falters in his faith, his ability to lead is marred. James calls him a double-minded man and unstable in all his ways (James 1:6-7).

But the word *faith* here is the Greek word *pistis*, which in this verse conveys more than faith alone but carries the idea of a person who is faithful, reliable, loyal, steadfast and has unwavering convictions.

When Paul wrote to Timothy, his young apprentice,

he urged him to choose leaders who were faithful men of deep conviction (2 Timothy 2:2). Ed Cole used to say, "Loyalty is the virtue of the faithful."

Faithfulness is a part of the eternal nature of God. The Bible stresses that God is faithful (1 Corinthians 1:9) and utterly dependable. The Bible says, "God is not a man, that he should lie, nor a son of man, that he should change his mind" (Numbers 23:19 ESV). Jesus Himself is "the same yesterday, today, and forever" (Hebrews 13:8 NKJV).

If this unchanging, constant, stable, unwavering behavior is the nature of God Himself, it shouldn't surprise us that Paul adds it as one of the key ingredients of how a real man acts. But the word that really jumps out at me is the word "convictions" because I believe it creates the framework for strong faith. The Message Bible uses the word convictions, which is a better translation of the word *pistis*. This is important because how can any man act like a man by God's standards without deep, strong, hard-core, godly convictions?

Ed Cole would say, "Be a man of convictions and not preferences because convictions always grow stronger under pressure while preferences grow weaker. Preferences are negotiable; convictions are non-negotiable. Why are convictions so important? Because they give purpose and purpose is one of the biggest factors in keeping men out of trouble! Jesus' convictions dominated His life. His primary conviction focused on doing the Father's will. This produced a deep awareness of His life's purpose and kept Him from the distraction of Satan's temptations. Pastor Mike Hayes says, "Men don't have a pornography problem; they have a purpose problem." I believe as long as I hold on to my convictions and have a purpose in God, I stay out of trouble. When I don't, I get into a lot of trouble! Pastor Erwin MacManus once said, "In the absence of clear purpose, we become addicted to the habitual performance of trivial and mundane."

Pajamas for Armor

A perfect example of this is King David. As long as David focused on his purpose, he stayed out of trouble, but when he lost focus of his convictions, he made one of the biggest mistakes of his life. When we first read of him, he is extraordinarily loyal. When he meets Prince Jonathan, he and Jonathan become covenant friends for life. When Jonathan's dad, King Saul, becomes jealous of David and tries to kill him, David still remains loyal. His convictions are so strong that once when he has a chance to kill Saul in a cave while the king relieves himself, David, instead, cuts off a piece of his robe and later becomes convicted in his heart for doing that. We read of him not even drinking the water that his faithful men bring to him from his favorite well in Bethel retrieved from behind enemy lines.

But later, when we see him on the rooftop of his palace playing peeping Tom with Bathsheba, we see how far he had fallen. What happened? The Bible records something very important, I believe, and it gives us insight into his fall from conviction to conniving and to eventual murder.

> *"It happened in the spring of the year, at the time when kings go out to battle, that David sent Joab and his servants with him, and all Israel; and they destroyed the people of Ammon and besieged Rabbah. But David remained at Jerusalem. Then it happened one evening that David arose from his bed and walked on the roof of the king's house. And from the roof, he saw a woman bathing, and the woman was very beautiful to behold. So David sent and inquired about the woman. And someone said, 'Is this not*

Bathsheba, the daughter of Eliam, the wife of Uriah the Hittite?' Then David sent messengers, and took her, and she came to him, and he lay with her, for she was cleansed of her impurity; and she returned to her house. And the woman conceived; so she sent and told David, and said, 'I am with child'" (2 Samuel 11:1-5 NKJV).

Did you catch it? David was not in the battle. Why wasn't he in his wheelhouse? He's a warrior without a war. Why did David stay home from the battle? If we can answer this we may find out why some men are not in the battle or why some have withdrawn from the battle entirely. One of my mentors, Pastor Jimmy Evans, has a sermon that we use at our retreats called "Every Great Man." In it he teaches a lot about both David's shortcomings and greatness. It has transformed my life and thousands of men around the country. He says that one of the possible reasons David lost his loyalty and convictions for battle was that he might have fallen into the belief that success had earned him the right to rest and retire from the battlefield. If this is true David must have had American blood in him! I say this because this is the proverbial thinking in America. America has a perverted view of success and retirement. The thinking is to make money so you can retire and drink Mai-Tais and drive a golf cart in Florida or own a yacht with beautiful girls around you. Yet, there is nothing in the Bible to support this view of success and retirement. In practice, retirement and a life of leisure cause misery, perversion, and early death. Whenever we exchange our armor for clothing of leisure like pajamas, we will experience drama in our pajamas.

Now, don't get me wrong; there is nothing wrong with saving money and retiring from a company or business, but at that point, we should re-fire for God and advance the kingdom. Pastor Mike Hayes did exactly that. He retired from the church he pastored for forty years, put his son in charge, and re-fired to start the National Center for Renewal on Capitol Hill. He now ministers to the leaders of our country. I know men who are working hard to retire early so they can focus on missions for the rest of their lives.

Wired for War

Men, we are wired for war; it's in our DNA. Genesis says, "So God created man in His own image; in the image of God He created him; male and female He created them. Then God blessed them, and God said to them, 'Be fruitful and multiply; fill the earth and subdue it; have dominion over the fish of the sea, over the birds of the air, and over every living thing that moves on the earth'" (Genesis 1:27-28 NKJV). The word *subdue* is a violent word in the Hebrew language. It means to subjugate by force. It says in Matthew, "From the days of John the Baptist until now, the kingdom of heaven has been forcefully advancing, and forceful men lay hold of it" (Matthew 11:12 NIV).

This is why we need to engage in this battle! I'm talking about the greatest battle of all! The battle over the souls of men! The battle of where people will spend eternity! The battle over heaven or hell! The battle over truth! The battle over the Word of God spread around the world! It's the only thing worthy of our lives because He is the only thing worthy of our lives! It's a good thing we are wired for war because we're smack in the middle of the biggest one ever!

The only thing worse than not fighting in this battle is fighting the wrong battle. You do not want your personal experience to reflect that you lived your whole life fighting for money, prestige, and power—or whatever — only to find out at the end your life it was a waste and was all for nothing. You do not want to conclude that the power you thought you had was powerless. But when you spend your life for God, every breath you breathe is spent for eternity. It's the only thing that matters and the only thing that will fulfill you. At the end of human history, Jesus Christ will have the rightful claim to all glory and dominion. "And from Jesus Christ, the faithful witness, the firstborn from the dead, and the ruler over the kings of the earth. To Him who loved us and washed us from our sins in His own blood, and has made us kings and priests to His God and Father, to Him be glory and dominion forever and ever. Amen!" (Revelation 1:5-6 NKJV).

Devil Killers

We are devil-killers and Satan doesn't want us to know that. We are not just designed for battle; we are designed and wired to win the battle. There is no battle we should lose. To lose strikes at the very spirit of a man, because we know we are designed for victory. We know we are designed for greatness! Here's the truth about the battle: no man can avoid it. You are either a warrior fighting or you are a captive (P.O.W.).

Years ago, I used to go on vacations with my family, and that was great, but the only problem is I would take a vacation from everything: the Bible, praying, church—everything. I would come home more tired than when I left. We can't retire from the battle or take a vacation from it because the devil doesn't take a vacation. When we surrender or won't fight for our family, then all those under our authority suffer. The punishment for David's sin spread to his entire family and all Israel! There is no such thing as private sin. At my men's retreats, I often hear men say about pornography, "My sin is my sin; it doesn't involve anyone else." But that's not true. It is what you're not doing that is just as bad or worse. You're not praying, you're not seeking God, and you're not reading the Word. The sin of omission is just as deadly as the sin of commission. Have you ever wondered what would have happened to Israel if David hadn't shown up and defeated Goliath? The same thing that would happen to your family if the devil defeats you. They will all become slaves to him. What I am saying is that the secret to true peace and rest is in warfare, not retirement.

Some think David stayed home because he was burnt out—tired of fighting. That can't be, because the

Bible says, "It was the season for kings to go to war," indicating there was a season kings did not go to war. It wasn't like David was too tired to fight; he just had a long restful winter. God won't push us too far or make us fight without rest — but when it's time to war — we must war! It wasn't that God asked too much of him. David was just irresponsible. David prospered and enjoyed rest as long as he lived by his convictions and fulfilled his purpose in battle.

The premise of John Eldridge's *Wild at Heart* book is that we are warriors who have forgotten who we are and have become tame. We lost conviction! Many of us have paid a great price because our fathers wouldn't fight or got taken out altogether by sin. Another possible answer as to why David stayed home was that he had already spotted Bathsheba and was waiting for an opportunity. I think this is a very high possibility because of how it all played out. I believe if the enemy can't take you out in battle with a bullet, he will try to take you out with a Bathsheba. Lack of conviction and sin take many men out of the battle; it almost kept me out and almost took me out!

Today, faithfulness, loyalty and godly convictions are core values in my life, but they weren't always. I'm ashamed to say that when I was younger and newly married, I was not faithful. I couldn't stay faithful to a woman if my life depended on it. It was ingrained in me by my father. According to him, it was just not something a real man did. You see, the Brazilian culture, like many Latin cultures, reeked with womanizing and promiscuous lifestyles. There is a saying in the Latin world of men. "Big house, small house" indicates a mistress on the side. I was raised under this kind of thinking, and it was wrong. It wasn't until the Lord got ahold of my heart and I repented and committed to becoming a faithful man that things changed. It was too late to save my first marriage, but when God gave me another chance, I went to war! Today I'm happily married and have been faithful to my wife, Misty, for thirty years and counting.

David's Bathsheba compromise caused more pain than any battle he had ever fought. Sin always delivers the opposite of what it promises. Sin will always cost you more than you want to pay; take you further than you want to go; and keep you longer than you want to stay. Nathan, his faithful friend and prophet, gave him the bad news, "Now, the sword will never depart from your house."

Whenever I go home to visit my family, I ultimately run into old friends still living in the world, and I'm always awestruck regarding how worn and tired they look. An old sinner's face tells the truth about sin. It promises what it cannot deliver, and it sucks the life out of you. The face of an old soldier with a deep conviction in God's army is where the joy is.

10

Men of Courage

"Act like men and be courageous!"

(1 Corinthians 16:13 AMP).

"Courage is the first of human qualities because it is the quality which guarantees all others."

—Winston Churchill

G od mentioned courage 638 times in the Bible. You know why? Because God knows courageous people will make the difference in this world. During the 1964 war between Malaysia and Indonesia, there existed a group of men called Gurkhas. It is a term for elite British Army units composed of Nepalese soldiers from Nepal. They were asked if they were willing to jump from transport planes into a combat zone if the need arose. The Gurkhas had the right to turn down the request because they had never been trained as paratroopers. Now, the Gurkhas usually agreed to anything, but on this occasion, they rejected the plan. But the next day one of their leaders sought out the British officer who made the request and said they had discussed the matter further and would be prepared to jump under certain conditions. "What are they?" asked the British Officer. The Gurkhas told him they would jump if the land were marshy or reasonably soft with no rocky outcrops because they were inexperienced in falling. The British officer considered this and said that the dropping areas would almost certainly be over the jungle, and there would not be rocky outcrops. Was there anything else? "Yes," said the Gurkhas, "we want the plane to fly as slowly as possible and no more than one hundred feet high. The British officer pointed out that the planes always flew as slowly as possible when dropping troops, but to jump from one-hundred feet was impossible because the parachutes would not open in time from that height. "Oh," said the Gurkhas, "that's alright, then. We'll jump with parachutes any-where. You didn't mention parachutes before!" Now that is what I call courage and commitment!

Courage like this is hard to find these days, and I think it's because courage is one of those words so adulterated and twisted by our modern culture that it's tough to get a handle on what it really means. Men are told that courage means fearlessness, taking risks or embracing some type of danger as in the story we just read. But the truth is courage can look different to many people. Courage can be standing up to your married boss who is living a life of immorality with a woman employee. I had a friend who did exactly that, and his boss repented and "got right." Courage can mean your walking away from a relationship with a girlfriend because you are unevenly yoked, as the Bible calls it, which basically means she is not as committed or devoted to God.

I knew a young man who I once mentored who reached that very decision with his girlfriend. She was dragging him down and pulling him away from God. He came to me with tears in his eyes asking me, "What do I do?" He had entered a sexual relationship with her and now had a "soul tie" with her and felt trapped. She also was his first real love, and he was afraid to lose her. I encouraged him that if he would honor God in this relationship, God would honor him. He walked away from her and today is married to a godly woman, has three wonderful kids, and is in full-time ministry.

It took courage to do that. Courage could be a young man joining the military, so he can get out of a small-town mindset and chase a future. Courage could mean getting up every morning to go to a job you hate but working hard anyway because it supports your family. Courage could be you telling your pals, "Hey, I can't do this stuff anymore, it's just not right," and walking away. Courage could be you telling your band of brothers, "Hey, I'm struggling again with my past addictions, and I need prayer." Courage could be falling on your knees to ask Christ into your heart.

I had a roommate in California who was dreaming of breaking into the bodybuilding world as I had done. He saw me running around with all these gorgeous girls, money and fame knocking down my door, and then I suddenly walked away from it all. He asked me what in the world I was thinking. He would give his left nut to have half of what I had. I told him God's plan for my life was more important than my plan. He laughed and told me I was crazy. It took courage for me to pursue God's plan, but here I am.

We need to embrace true courage. You know, taking action despite your fear. Doing something you're afraid of because that thing is more important and certainly more important than your fear. It might include attending a retreat like the ones we put on (*The Return*) and dealing with junk in your trunk. I have always liked John Wayne's quote about courage, "Courage is when you're scared out of your mind, but you saddle up anyway."

Fear of Failure

Whenever you hear the word "courage" in the Bible, you often hear the word "strong" attached to it. The reason is because there's a difference between strength and courage. When the Bible speaks of strength, it's more the physically enduring aspect of a person. When it speaks of courage, it points to the nerve that inspires strength to take action. They are often paired together because, like a kite, an opposing wind raises it higher. But let's go back to the life of King David and see it in action, especially as a backdrop to this subject of fear, because it could be another possible reason David stayed home from war. He had lost his nerve. Fear never originates with God, and it always leads to wrong decisions we regret. We all have fears we have to face and overcome if we are going to succeed with God. The most common fear I hear all the time is the fear of failure. I believe the primary root of this fear is the fear that "I am inadequate to the assignment." Almost all fears come down to a question of identity. 'Am I enough? Do I have what it takes?' The secondary root of our fears is the fear that 'if I become known, then it reveals who I really am.' In other words, 'if I strip down and become naked before you, will you still love me? If you really knew me and my limitations, would you reject me, and would I be disqualified and pushed away from the opportunity?'

These two fears are at the root of most fears, and if not dealt with, will paralyze, or worse, sabotage your calling. Here is the truth. You are enough, and the clearer you are about your identity the more freedom you will have from the weight of unresolved doubts and negative narratives that the enemy has stuffed into your head and that spills out under pressure. The more aware you are of where the enemy hits you, the easier it is for you to dismantle the lie by proclaiming the truth. We say this a lot at our retreats, "If a lie holds you captive then only truth can set you free." One thing I have learned about courage in my own life is that it doesn't mean you don't feel fear. It means you act beyond it! The first prophecy ever spoken over me came by the late Dick Mills. I will never forget it; he said, "You will be an evangelist, I see you leading what seems like the sands of the seashore, too many to count, to the Lord! Only be strong and courageous…go get them, tiger."

Which brings me to another understanding of courage that a friend of mine, Ryan Leak, who attended one of my retreats, said: "Courage is not a suggestion of God but a command right up there with 'Do not steal. Do not kill. Do not murder." He has a point because in Joshua 1:9 God says, "Have I not commanded you? Be strong and courageous." Leak when on to say, "He can command us to be courageous because He's the insurance policy on our success. God is not encouraging us to be strong and courageous because we're great, but because He's great."

I couldn't agree more. All that I have accomplished is because He has empowered me. He has given me the courage to do what I do. There is no one more courageous than the Holy Spirit, and when we ask Him to live in us, we are connected to the power plant of heaven. There is nothing we cannot do.

Battles Make Men

The bottom line is this: we can guess all day long why David stayed home from the battlefield, but this we know — David's rise to greatness stopped the minute he withdrew from the battlefield, and his problems began. Let's get real. All of us have at one point or another dealt with — and many are still dealing with — the lure of worldliness and the images of retirement, independence, prosperity, and the easy life. They are very alluring to us. Lust, the desire for sexual pleasure and sexual excitement beyond what marriage offers, is a great tool and lie of the enemy, and many have fallen for it. But I believe fear is Satan's greatest weapon. It has demoralized and taken out more men than anything else. We fear facing our failures and doubts about entering the battle and giving it all to God. More anointing or prophetic words will not do the trick, but what will is to act boldly and courageously on the truth that has already been proclaimed about you. This is what our retreats focus on, to help men identify the lies and fears and move them toward truth in the Word and what it says about them. This is where purpose is once again ignited with courage. Someone once said, "Courage is not the absence of fear, but it's the belief of something greater." However, the real problems we deal with are not the ones I listed in the last chapters; the real problem is that we're not in the battle! As a warrior, David had unbelievable courage. On the battlefield he took on a giant—Goliath. In the battlefield he had incredible integrity; he would not attack King Saul, he would not drink water his men put their lives on the line to retrieve. On the battlefield he is an impeccable example of a courageous and "integras" man.

Integras Men

Integras is the Latin word from which we get integrity, which means soundness, wholeness or entirety. Steven Mansfield in his book *Manly Men* shares that this word was often used during inspection rituals in the army of ancient Rome. When a commander would walk the line of his army, inspecting each man to confirm that he was fit for duty, he would walk by each, and they would slam their chest armor with their fist and yell, "Integras!" The commander would listen for strength of voice and the sound that armor emits when it's well-kept and fitted. The two sounds—the man's voice and the condition of his armor—confirmed the integrity of the soldier fit for battle. On the rooftop, David had lost his integras.

Men without Chest

On the rooftop David was a man without a chest. Let me explain. C.S. Lewis likened the properly ordered soul to the human body: the head (reason) must rule the belly (the sensual appetites) through the chest (character and spirit). The chest is the indispensable liaison between reason and the appetite. Without a strong "chest," men would succumb to excuses, relativism, and compromise. Lewis called those with no character or integrity, "men without chests." David stole one of his most faithful soldiers' wives, committed adultery with her, and then had that soldier killed in battle to cover his sin. David's problem on the rooftop was not a temptation problem as much as a location problem. What he did with Bathsheba wouldn't have happened if he had been where he should have been: at the battle!

Rooftop Battle

My first rooftop battle for me came one night while living in Pasadena, California trying to get my career back on track. I'd gotten discouraged by some opportunities that didn't pan out in ministry, so I went back to what I knew. I quickly built up some clientele and had a few movies and modeling opportunities lined up. I had contracts and magazines wanting me. All was going well except for this nagging, gnawing feeling in my gut that God had something different planned for me. I went to my rooftop where I liked to pray and there the battle began.

On one side I heard the devil saying all the nice things. He showed me all the accolades and money and the girls that wanted me. He showed me flashes of my success and how I was gifted and talented for what I was doing and that the sky was the limit. On the other side, I heard God telling me about the calling to a greater life; one of sacrifice and pain but one which would have eternal ramifications on many lives. He assured me He had gifted me for this work, and that when I felt inadequate, it would always cause me to rely on Him. I knew this was the moment and if I chose to stay on the rooftop and not to go to battle, I would forever regret it. I cried out to God, "What if your plan doesn't work? What if I fail?" That's when He said something I will never forget, "A God-plan never fails, a man-plan always will." My friend, Tim Story, coined a phrase, "There's a good idea, and there's a God idea. A good idea *may* come to pass, but a God idea *must* come to pass." I chose the God-idea, the God-plan, the battlefield, and I am glad I did.

Our issues of worldliness, lust, and fear cannot find a successful resolve on the rooftop. Such things can only be settled on the battlefield. "For though we walk in the flesh, we do not war according to the flesh. For the weapons of our warfare are not carnal but mighty in God for pulling down strongholds, casting down arguments and every high thing that exalts itself against the knowledge of God, bringing every thought into captivity to the obedience of Christ, and being ready to punish all disobedience when your obedience is fulfilled" (2 Corinthians 10:3-6 NKJV).

"Blessed is the man who walks not in the counsel of the ungodly, nor stands in the path of sinners, nor sits in the seat of the scornful; but his delight is in the law of the LORD, and in His law, he meditates day and night. He shall be like a tree planted by the rivers of water, that brings forth its fruit in its season, whose leaf also shall not wither; and whatever he does shall prosper" (Psalm 1:1-3 NKJV).

The only lasting answer to lust and pornography is to war for your thoughts and win! This mind we have is a phenomenal piece of hardware. But we have a virus called sin and the Bible is a virus-killing program. Beyond ourselves, the battlefield stretches into our marriages and families, and into our communities and nations. The real warrior doesn't just fight for himself; he fights for others. The rooftop can corrupt the best in all of us, but the battlefield can bring it back — it did for David. Rooftop men will justify what a warrior won't. They do what warriors find detestable. Rooftop men only think of themselves and their desires. Every man needs to come to this decision: the rooftop of your pleasure or the battlefield of God's pleasure. It's time to enter the battlefield. You are a winning warrior and it's where you belong. It's the answer to the problem the rooftop creates. Remember this. Your problems will not go away on the rooftop, they will only multiply. Every courageous man chooses the battlefield because only the battlefield can produce a true *Andrizo man*!

11

Men of Strength

"Act like men and be courageous; grow in strength!"
(1 Corinthians 16:13 AMP).

"You are their glorious strength. It pleases you to make us strong"
(Psalms 89:17 NLT).

"Do not pray for easier lives. Pray to be stronger men."
—John F. Kennedy

"Though Satan makes strong men weak, God is in the business of making weak men strong."
—Craig Groeschel

John G. Lake used to say; "This is a strong man's gospel." I like that because I believe it with all my heart. But there was a time when I didn't understand true strength. I thought it was all physical but quickly learned it was much, much more! Webster's Dictionary defines strength as, "The quality or state of being strong, the capacity for exertion or endurance. The power to resist a negative force or attack." I noticed whenever the Bible mentions strength, it usually speaks of moral strength, inner strength, and character—not the physical. This is what Paul conveys to the Andrizo men he is trying to raise up in Corinth.

To Empower

Andrizo fully spelled out in Greek is *andrizomi*. Pete Tsininos, a Greek friend, told me that when you break down the word an-drizo-mi you get "Man-poured-into me." Now, that gets interesting because isn't that exactly what God did to us when He breathed life into us?

"Then the LORD God formed a man from the dust of the ground and breathed into his nostrils the breath of life, and the man became a living being" (Geneses 2:7 NIV).

Isn't that what Jesus did to His disciples and then told them to do the same. "And with that he breathed on them and said, 'Receive the Holy Spirit'" (John 20:22 NIV). His last words to us were to, "go into all the world and make disciples..." (Matthew 28:19).

After we are empowered by the Holy Spirit, we are to empower others. Paul is telling us this by the very word he used in the Greek. The word here for strong in the Greek is *krataihoo* from the root word *krataios,* which means more than just physical strength alone, but empowering strength. Men, this is talking about more than might or vigor—it's about discipleship, mentoring, pouring into other men, empowering others! As I said earlier, only true masculinity can bestow true masculinity. That is why ministries like *The Return, Heroes Return* and *The Awakening* are important because they empower!

One of the greatest things you can do is mentor and be mentored. We should always position ourselves with one hand that reaches to where others pull us up and the other hand that reaches down to pull others up. It's the picture of what I think King Solomon meant when he said, "A threefold cord is not quickly broken" (Ecclesiastes 4:12 NKJV).

The Hit List

David did this with Solomon. In First Kings, David is on his deathbed, and he has his young son summoned to his bedside where he says,

"I go the way of all the earth; be strong, therefore, and prove yourself a man. And keep the charge of the LORD your God: to walk in His ways, to keep His statutes, His commandments, His judgments, and His testimonies, as it is written in the Law of Moses, that you may prosper in all that you do and wherever you turn, that the LORD may fulfill His word which He spoke concerning me, saying, 'If your sons take heed to their way, to walk before Me in truth with all their heart and with all their soul,' He said, 'you shall not lack a man on the throne of Israel'" (1 Kings 2:2-4 NKJV).

This is David's last attempt to pour qualities of manhood into his young son, Solomon, who is about to take over the throne. And what are the first words he uses? He uses the Hebrew word *chazaq*, which as I mentioned ealier, is the equivalence of the Greek word Andrizo. How cool is that? David was an *Andrizo* man, and an *Andrizo* man bestows strength. That is the true nature of the word *Andrizo*. It's not so much what you are on the outside but what has been poured into you on the inside. Your manhood then finds its greatest fulfillment in what you possess to pour out upon others.

David also knows his son had never faced a battlefield experience. Solomon grew up during peacetime and never knew the inside of a cave or a wielded sword. He knows his son needs some warrior spirit poured into him. David also knows the enemy is near. As a matter of fact, his next statement to Solomon is like a scene taken right out of *The Godfather*. It's a hit list if I ever saw one. I can practically hear the violin in the background as he speaks it.

"Moreover, you know also what Joab the son of Zeruiah did to me, and what he did to the two commanders of the armies of Israel, to Abner, the son of Ner and Amasa the son of Jether, whom he killed. And he shed the blood of war in peacetime and put the blood of war on his belt that was around his waist, and on his sandals, that were on his feet. Therefore, do according to your wisdom, and do not let his gray hair go down to the grave in peace. But show kindness to the sons of Barzillai the Gileadite, and let them be among those who eat at your table, for so they came to me when I fled from Absalom your brother. And see, you have with you Shimei the son of Gera, a Benjamite from Bahurim, who cursed

me with a malicious curse in the day when I went to Mahanaim. But he came down to meet me at the Jordan, and I swore to him by the LORD, saying, 'I will not put you to death with the sword.' Now, therefore, do not hold him guiltless, for you are a wise man and know what you ought to do to him; but bring his gray hair down to the grave with blood" (1 Kings 2:5-9 NKJV).

"You are a wise man and know what you ought to do." The word "do" in Hebrew means to *execute, to advance or fight for.* In other words, David tells him not to coexist with the enemy. An Andrizo man does not play with the enemy; instead, he knocks his lights out! Cuts off his stinking head! This is the same thing God told Moses and Joshua when conquering the Promised Land.

The Poser

When I was a kid my cousin, Emanuel, and I were jumped by a several larger kids who thought we had flipped them off. My cousin had studied a little karate and tried to scare them by doing a Bruce Lee impersonation and spun a stick around like a Samarian sword. When he finished his little charade, the stick snapped and so did our bones as the boys jumped on us. Posing never works. Eventually you will be called out. Your stick won't hold up and the enemy knows it. There is a hilarious story in the Bible of some men who learned this lesson the hard way. They were a team of brothers known as the "Seven Sons of Sceva." One day they decided to try to cast out some evil spirits from a man by saying, "I command you by Jesus, whom Paul preaches, to come out!" The evil spirit replied, "I know Jesus, and I know Paul. But who are you?" And he jumped on them and beat their pants off. I'm not kidding you. It literally says they ran out of the house naked and bleeding (Acts 19:13-15). You know what this tells me? The Devil knows the difference! So, we better know the difference!

The weak man, the poser, will surface when push comes to shove. In the book of Judges, there is a story of another son. This time it's Gideon's son. They had just defeated the enemy and were in hot pursuit of the kings of the army. When they finally catch them, Gideon has them tied up and lays them on the ground and puts his foot on their necks. Then he calls out his young son to rise and kill them. Gideon tries to pour his strength into his young son but he's a poser. "And he said to Jether his firstborn, 'Rise, kill them!' But the youth would not draw his sword; for he was afraid, because he was still a youth. So Zebah and Zalmunna said, 'Rise yourself, and kill us; for as a man is, so is his strength.' So, Gideon arose and killed Zebah and Zalmunna, and took the crescent ornaments that were on their camels' necks" (Judges 8:20-21 NKJV).

A poser is someone all dressed up, got a sword and some armor, but no strength, no courage, no Andrizo!

Someone once said, "The true virtue of strength is to love, to give of oneself and to protect!" Which leads me to the final virtue and, according to God, the greatest of all.

Men of Compassion

"Let everything you do be done in love"

(1 Corinthians 16:14 NLT).

"Compassion will cure more sins than condemnation."

—Henry Ward Beecher

"Faults are thick where love is thin."   —Unknown

"Whoever pursues righteousness and unfailing love will find life, righteousness, and honor"

(Proverbs 21:21 NLT).

Funny Love

I find it interesting that Paul wraps this manhood deal with love. The Greek word for "love" as used in this passage is *"agape."* It carries the connotation of a moral preference or preferred love of God that we are to live out. It speaks of benevolence, good will, charity, and esteeming others above self. This is why I choose the word compassion to best describe it. Also, the word "love" has been hijacked and watered down to the point that many don't take it seriously. How many times has someone said they love you while "sticking a knife in your back?" As a pastor, I have had firsthand experience in this. People say, "I love you, Pastor," and the next thing they do is leave the church over some offence, and they begin to slander you, never once coming to you and trying to work things out. You hear things like, "I love my dog; I love my job; I love my car; I love; I love" But do they really? I call it funny love. That's why I don't throw around the word "love" unless I truly mean it.

Moved by Compassion

Compassion is a truly deep concept with dimension. First, it has the word "passion" in it, and I like that because it takes passion in order to love. Second, every time Jesus loved, He was moved by compassion. In the book of Matthew, in the last verse of chapter nine, Jesus was having an awesome day teaching, preaching, and healing all who were sick. Most ministers I know, including me, would have been satisfied with such a great day. Not Jesus! Something moved Him even more than just preaching a good word and healing the sick. The Bible says, "But when He *saw* the multitudes, He was moved with compassion for them, because they were *weary* and scattered, like sheep having no shepherd" (Matthew 9:35-36 NKJV).

Moved by compassion for what? The word *saw* there means to perceive, understand, consider, or inspect. The word *weary* means to be harassed or thrown aside by society. In other words – Jesus got a closer look at the discontented, discombobulated, and beaten down condition of the people, and His heart broke for them. When was the last time that happened to you?

This used to happen to me often when I was on the road, traveling as a missionary evangelist. Once while in Mexico City with James Roberson, I couldn't stop praying for the people at the altar. People were getting saved and healed. A tumor melted before my eyes as I prayed for this young woman. I wept with compassion for the desperation of the people to the point where security had to be called to pull me out because of the danger of being crushed by the crowd. Another time in Brazil, I was preaching in my parents' hometown in a large soccer stadium. When I gave the invitation for people to receive Christ, the avalanche of souls coming down was overwhelming, and I broke down weeping saying, "God, there are so many." Also, in Russia, I was preaching and seeing thousands coming to Christ but weeping over the ones that didn't. Compassion does that to you.

As an Andrizo man, it's important that we slow down in life and look around to SEE what people are going through and do what we can to help. The whole story of the Good Samaritan that Jesus taught in Luke 10:25-37 was in response to a question posed to him about charity. A religious teacher asked him,

"Who is my neighbor?"
"Whom should I help?"
"Whom should I care for?"
"Whom am I obliged to?"

Jesus takes the opportunity to teach through this beautiful story. First, you must understand - Jesus didn't simply pull this parable out of a hat. He used a well-known road. The road in the story was one of the steepest and most treacherous roads — the road from

Jerusalem to Jericho. It stretched out about eighteen miles east of Jerusalem. Its nickname was *"The Bloody Way"* because of its infestation of bandits. Lack of compassion is often easy to justify even though it is never right. The man's question to Jesus, though not sincere, suggests several things:

There must be some to whom the obligation to love does not apply – thus meriting a limit to our duty of caring.

He emphasizes the worthiness of the object of love rather than the attitude of the one who is to do the loving.

"True love" does not consider the worth of its object, but it simply responds to human need out of compassion. There was a deep hatred between Jews and Samaritans. Jews considered Samaritans a mongrel race with a polluted religion. The Jews saw themselves as pure descendants of Abraham, while Samaritans were a mixed race that intermarried during the exile of Israel.

To this teacher of the law that asked Jesus the question, the person least likely to act correctly would be a

Samaritan. In fact, if you notice, he couldn't even bring himself to say "Samaritan" in his answer to Jesus' question. This expert, professional religionist's attitude betrayed the very law that he quoted from (Deut. 6:5 –Lev. 19:18 ...*to love God and thy neighbor*). Jesus threw the question back at the man but changed the emphasis. "It is not, "Who was the neighbor?" as much as it is "Who proved to be the neighbor?" Jesus had to set the record straight for the sake of the bystanders listening. So, he pulled the rug out from this man's hypocrisy. He took that low compassion way of thinking and elevated it to the high compassion thinking of God! The Apostle John writes of this, "But whoso hath this world's good, and seeth his brother have need, and shutteth up his bowels of compassion from him, how dwelleth the love of God in him?" (1 John 3:17 KJV).

Forgive me if I sound a little crass here, but I want to tell you exactly why the Holy Spirit chose this word *splocknitzomy* ("bowels") to describe Jesus' compassion. Let's think about biology, specifically about physiology, for a moment. What happens when a person's bowels move? The movement of the bowels produce action and change. Likewise, when the human spirit is deeply touched and moved by the need of another person, it causes a movement, a change, or a release of divine power to surge from deep within the person to reach out and meet the needs of the other individuals. This is why whenever Jesus was "moved by compassion," His actions always resulted in people being healed, delivered, fed, etc. There is a difference between passion and compassion. Passion is a human emotion that can be affected by circumstances; compassion is divine, it comes from deep within.

Wherever you live, there are needy people close by. There is no good reason for refusing to help. But more critical than simply helping is "why you are helping." There is no doubt that the compassion Jesus talks about produces action, but its actions are birthed out of a deep love for people. Deuteronomy 15:7-8 (NLT) says, "But if there are any poor Israelites in your towns when you arrive in the land the LORD your God is giving you, do not be hard-hearted or tightfisted toward them. Instead, be generous and lend them whatever they need." Scriptures like this started gnawing at my lack of compassion. This is why it is challenging for me to drive or walk by a person in need today and not give something. Charity is not simply the virtue of the hands but also of the heart. Love is more than what we say and do; it is what we are. I like the ancient legend about the monk who found a precious stone, a precious jewel. A short time later, the monk met a traveler who said he was hungry and asked the monk if he would share some of his provisions. When the monk opened his bag, the traveler saw the precious stone and, on an impulse asked the monk if he could have it. Amazingly, the monk gave the traveler the stone. The traveler departed quickly, overjoyed with his new possession. However, a few days later, he came back, searching for the monk. He returned the stone to the monk and made a request: "Please give me something more valuable, more precious than this stone. Please give me that which enabled you to give me this precious stone!"

Paul said, "And though I bestow all my goods to feed the poor, and though I give my body to be burned, and have not charity, (agape – deep affection) it profiteth me nothing" (1 Corinthians 13:3 KJV). Paul is saying this from a heart that had been transformed by the Spirit of God. When Paul first appeared in scripture, he had a lot of passion but lacked compassion. He was passionate about the things "of God" but not "for God." In the book of Acts, Paul cheered on and even watched the coats of the individuals who stoned Stephen, the disciple (Act 7:58, 8:1).

In Acts, chapter nine, Paul is breathing more threats and murder against the church when he is converted on the road to Damascus. God directed his misguided passion and gave him a great compassion for people that the church he was raised in thumbed their noses at. He is a major influence in us Gentiles coming to know Christ. If it weren't for Paul's love, we wouldn't have three-quarters of the New Testament written. So, it's ironic that Paul is the one God chose to write the love chapter of 1 Corinthians 13. My point is, Paul, like many of us, had to learn what authentic love was.

Another great example of this love transformation is Peter. Peter was a beloved disciple of Christ, but he lacked love and compassion for God's people. He was erratic. One minute he was announcing that he would die for Christ and never abandon him; the next minute he was denying him three times. One minute he was pulling out a sword to defend Jesus; the next minute he was running for his life.

After the resurrection, Jesus shows up at the Sea of Galilee where Peter had reverted to his former life as a fisherman. Jesus arrives at the beach and begins to cook breakfast for him and asks him three times if he loves him. The first two times Peter's answers do not reflect committed love. On the last time, Peter answers with the *agape* love that Paul talks about in 1 Corinthians 16:14. That *agape* love changed everything. His life was marked, not only by passion, but by compassion for all people, Jews and Gentiles alike. Agape love made the difference in Paul's life. It made the difference in Peter's life. Importantly, it will make the difference in your life. This is why Paul added it to the distinctive and authentic manhood list.

We were created in God's image to do basically two things: to love God and to love people. Life is primarily about love. In order to love others, we first need to understand and feel how much God loves us. We need to reach an understanding of how God loves us completely and unconditionally. We need to become secure in the truth that we cannot make God stop loving us. Once we're secure inside God's unconditional love, we'll start cutting other people slack. We won't be as angry as before. We'll be more patient, forgiving, merciful, and compassionate. George Washington Carver once said, "How far you go in life depends on your being tender with the young, compassionate with the aged, sympathetic with the striving, and tolerant of the weak and the strong. Because someday in life you will have been all of these." Paul said, "And regardless of what else you put on, wear love. It's your basic, all-purpose garment. Never be without it" (Colossians 3:14 MSG).

My Love Walk

I don't know about you, but for me the "love walk" has been one of the most difficult challenges of my Christian life. I didn't have good examples of love and compassion while growing up. I learned to "lust" after women, not "love" them. I learned that if you hurt me, I will hurt you. The first time I had to walk away from a fight was crazy hard, and I hated the fact it was so hard. While driving in traffic, a young punk cut me off and then commenced to flip me off. He then waved me over to the shoulder to fight. I was huge at the time and could fight well. As a matter of fact, I have never lost a fight in my life, and I was about to add to my perfect record. But the Holy Spirit arrested me and said drive on. It took me several miles and over an hour to calm down. God said to me later, "James, if you can't walk away from this now, which really is a little matter, you won't be able to walk away from it later when it's a big matter."

I had a friend who was part of my early "strength-feat" ministry who never got his temper under control. One day, while at a popular fast food restaurant drive-through, he allegedly got into an altercation with another driver behind him in line. This driver was a gang member. Instead of driving away, my friend's temper got the better of him, and he made an attempt to get out of the car. This cost him his life as the gang member shot my friend in the head. The deceased left behind a wife and five young kids.

Years ago, while on the road preaching, I was in a very dangerous, gang-infested town when I had another altercation in traffic. I stayed very calm and drove away. Later, God told me the car was full of gang members, and they had a murderous spirit; they wanted to kill me. The hairs on my arms stood up. Love had saved my life.

Notice how Paul bookends this manhood thing with vigilance and compassion. Both take an incredible amount of selflessness, and that is a hard thing for many, if not most, men. Let's face it, men, we can be some of the most selfish, self-centered, S.O.Bs on this earth. We can easily activate the "me, myself and I trinity" and not even see it. My self-centeredness in my early years cost me dearly.

Washing Feet

The greatest teacher of love I have ever had is my wife, Misty. Not that she is the most compassionate person – she has her moments – but she is the vessel and the example of the love of God that teaches me. During our dating months, leading up to our wedding, I began to have "cold feet." I was seriously thinking of postponing the wedding. Then it happened: Misty, not knowing the vacillation of my heart, walked into the room that I was sitting in and began washing my feet. I kept saying to her, "No, you don't want to do that," (mostly because my feet had been through a lot and stank). But she insisted, saying, "The Lord told me to."

That's when I remembered the request that I had asked of the Lord many years prior. After my earlier devastating divorce, I'd asked God to give me a sign to make sure I knew that next woman I married was the right one. I asked Him to have her wash my feet and specifically to start with my left foot. Why my left food? I have no idea, but it was what it was. I shared this with my pastor at the time, and he laughed at me and said that was dangerous because what if some unappealing woman that I have no attraction to came up and began washing my feet? So, I just laughed it off and forgot about it, until this Misty moment. God had heard my prayer, and even though it was silly and possibly dangerous, He had it done. There was Misty washing my feet, crying and silently praying and yes, she started with my left foot. Now, if you knew my wife, you would know how much of a miracle this was. She is not the foot-washing type. This was real love and obedience to God! Man, if I could just get her to obey me now!

Years later, when I first experienced a version of *The Return* retreat that I conduct for men called, "Quest," I had a life-transforming moment with the Father and later with my family. As I mentioned earlier, I have had the privilege of raising three girls. At first, I thought having all girls was payback for how badly I treated women in my younger years, but now I see it as a gift from God to teach me how to love. It tenderized me; it taught me to be gentle, loving and nurturing, yet strong. While on this retreat, God took control of my heart and freed me from many vices. He began to show me where I lacked compassion and where I had hardened my heart to people.

When I got home, I knew I had to *Andrizo Up* in front of my wife and children for all the years I was selfish, prideful, impatient, and hard. I asked them to sit on the couch, and one by one, I washed their feet and asked them to forgive me. I must admit, we had a cry fest, but the change it made was nothing short of a miracle. I began to love them as Christ intended. It transformed my marriage and my children. Today, my girls are doing great in college, serving God, and keeping a close relationship with their mother and me, but most of all they are compassion-driven. Recently, my oldest daughter was interviewed by "Compassion International," an organization that helps poor children around the world. That one moment of being moved with compassion and beginning to love my family as Christ loved the church changed my life and theirs. Love has that effect. That is why scripture says, "Love never fails!" Paul wrote a lot about love. I believe it's because, like me, he had to learn it. The Message translation says, "So, no matter what I say, what I believe, and what I do, I'm bankrupt without love" (1 Corinthians 13:8 MSG).

Men, the Word of God clearly tells us that God is

looking for men today who will stand in the gap for the sake of distinctive and authentic manhood and say, "Here I am, make me a man of vigilance, convictions, courage, strength, and compassion."

The son who returned to the path of the Father had a heart-change that every man must have. We must move beyond "give me" and become men who say, "Father make me." Make me an *ANDRIZO MAN!"*